How to Decorate Your Home Without Going Broke

How to Decorate Your Home Without Going Broke

by Barty Phillips

**Projects and Question and Answer Section
by Eleanor Van Zandt**

Doubleday and Company Inc.,
Garden City, New York 1975

Also published as How to Decorate Without Going Broke

Series Coordinator: John Mason
Design Director: Guenther Radtke
Picture Editor: Peter Cook
Editor: Eleanor Van Zandt
Copy Editor: Mitzi Bales
Research: Marian Pullen
Consultants: Beppie Harrison
             Jo Sandilands

This edition published in the
United States of America in 1975 by
Doubleday & Company Inc., New York
in association with Aldus Books Limited

Library of Congress Catalog Card
No. 74 10420

ISBN: 0 385 07043 8

© 1974 Aldus Books Limited, London

Printed and bound in Spain by
T.O.N.S.A. and Roner S.A.,
Crta. de Irun, Km. 12,450,
Madrid 34. Dep. Legal: S.S. 308/75

Contents

Decorating your home is one of the most satisfying forms of self-expression. It can also be one of the most expensive. Fortunately, though, you can cut costs in your decorating. You can do your own painting, make your own curtains, disguise ugly furniture. You can also shop sensibly, armed with basic facts about color schemes, carpets, and the other components of a decorating plan. In this book you'll find the basic knowledge you need for successful decorating, plus practical suggestions to help you stretch your decorating budget. A special projects section, and some questions and answers on specific decorating problems, will give you ideas for fixing up your own home.

What is a Home?

On the simplest level, a home is a shelter. It protects us from cold and damp, and provides a certain amount of privacy. Each culture interprets these needs in a different way—and builds houses accordingly.

Below: "The Neanderthal Encampment" is an artist's idea of how cavemen lived.

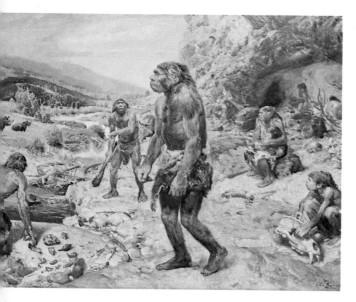

Above: a Zulu hut is made of twigs and branches woven together and thatched with grass, and can be shifted to another location.

Below: the only housing material available to an Eskimo is snow, packed into blocks.

Above: for these young Lapps, home is wherever the community pitches tents.

Above: this half-timbered manor house is typical of Elizabethan landowners' homes.

Above right: junks and sampans in Hong Kong's harbor serve as homes for thousands.

Below: several families live together in each of these striking Indonesian longhouses.

Above: this ultramodern Brazilian apartment was designed by Oskar Niemeyer.

On the Walls

Plain walls will keep out the cold adequately, but for centuries people have decorated their walls—sometimes with paint, sometimes with paper, tiles, or fabric.

Below: this Aboriginal cave painting in Australia was intended to quieten the spirits.

Bottom: dolphins adorn the walls in the Queen's apartments at Cnossus, Crete.

Above: this fresco in the Villa of Mysteries, Pompeii, is typical of the ancient wall paintings found in wealthy homes of that day.

Above: wall hangings decorated medieval castles, and helped to keep out drafts.

Right: painted tiles of Middle East design give opulence to this room in Leighton House, London, decorated in the late 1800's.

Below: these tiles in a Turkish mosque show Persian influence in their intricate design.

Below: hand-printed wallpaper designed by William Morris started a new trend in home decorating in late Victorian times.

Below right: the human element, in Pop Art form, decorates this wall and door.

Furniture Fun

We seldom think of furniture as amusing. As long as it's functional, and preferably handsome, it serves. Some designers, however, have produced furniture with an element of "play" about it. Some of their designs are beautiful; others are ... well, interesting.

Below: the curtained fourposter is a fun idea in bed design, but originally it had a very practical function—to keep out drafts.

Right: the Victorian taste for solid comfort and fanciful design produced some novel kinds of furniture, such as this three-seat sofa.

Below: the Rail Age comes to the dining room table—electrically run cars bring food from the kitchen, and are stopped where required. At bottom, a car brings on the fish.

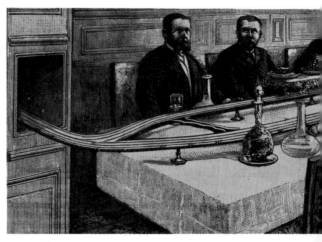

Left and above: sitting witty—a chair in the form of an enormous mouth, and a flock of make-believe sheep. The French sculptor who designed the sheep also did the huge seagull- and egg-shaped bed shown below.

The Fashionable Room

Every age and every culture has developed a distinctive style of interior to express its ideas of beauty and comfort. Today, we can adapt any of the past styles to give our modern rooms a feeling of traditional charm.

Right: this painting of "Le Dejeuner" ("the lunch") by Boucher depicts an elegant French home of the mid-18th century.

Below: "The Dinner Party," by Henry Sargent, shows a Boston interior of the early 1800's, furnished in formal neoclassic style.

Above: this Early American interior, part of the Henry Ford Museum, reflects the stark simplicity of 17th-century New England.
Left: the Royal Pavilion, Brighton, England, has some furniture in "the Chinese taste", popular in Europe in the 1700's.

Below left: this Art Nouveau bedroom is typical of this romantic, fanciful style.

Below: traditional Spanish architecture and furniture design in a new *hacienda*.

No law says a chair must have legs, or a mattress must have stuffing. Today, designers are expanding our ideas of what furniture is.

Below: home from foam—walls of burlap, wood, and wire, sprayed with foam.

Above: the water bed is the latest word in sleeping comfort. Good ones are equipped with a frame, and are electrically heated.

Right: the Retreat Pod offers a "return to the womb." Sound- and light-proof, it is upholstered inside for maximum comfort.

Below: furniture for children is becoming more and more imaginative. This giant dinosaur is for sitting, climbing, and playing on.

Above: the components of this conversation pit can be moved around as desired.

Right: see-through chair, made of inflatable cushions on a nearly invisible frame.

The Adventure of Decorating

1

Your home is your refuge, your castle. It's where you bring up your children, where you entertain your friends, where you eat, sleep, make love, work, and play. It's where you can kick off your shoes and relax; it's a retreat at times of stress.

Your home is also an extension of your own personality. Wherever you live—even if it's only in temporary furnished quarters—it should reflect your own taste, and the tastes of other members of the family. Even a plant, a few books, and a favorite poster will contribute something toward making the place yours, rather than just a place.

When it's a matter of planning a permanent home, the opportunities and the rewards are much greater. You can decide which colors you want to live with, which designs best express your idea of home.

Decorating your home takes time and a lot of thought, but it needn't require stacks of money. The ideas in this book are tailored to a moderate budget, and are intended to help you apportion your money wisely, avoiding both needless extravagance and false economy. It is inadvisable, for example, to buy the kind of carpet that will have to be replaced in nine months, but equally foolish to buy an expensive, long-wearing one for the bedroom, where a cheaper one would do.

This book will show you how you can save money by doing many jobs yourself instead of hiring someone to do them for you, and how you can create big effects with a small amount of money and some imagination. You'll discover that decorating on a limited budget is, in a sense, the most satisfying way to decorate, because it forces you to use your ingenuity.

With two to share the work, home decorating can be fun, as well as economical. These two have prepared the wall by filling in the cracks with plaster, and are about to enjoy the satisfaction of changing the room with fresh new color.

Left: your family's life-style will influence your decorating. If you have a husband who repairs machinery in the bed-room, you'll want to take this into consideration in planning your decorating —avoiding pale velvet pile carpeting, for example, and, instead, using some inexpensive scatter rugs.

Right: children's rooms should provide for their hobbies and rambunc-tious activities. Bunk beds are fun, leave more space for play. The ones shown here are equipped with large drawers for storing toys or bedding.

Before you start buying, establish your priorities, and your decorating philosophies. Unless you're living on your own, this will usually involve compromise. You may adore pink draperies and ruffled bedspreads, but don't force them on a husband who prefers cork walls and leather chairs. Find a style that appeals to both of you. Similarly, let your children choose the decor for their rooms, within reason. If they really want 10 kinds of patterned paper in their room, and it doesn't cost you any extra, why shouldn't they have it? They can paint over it next year without breaking the bank.

An important part of your planning is apportioning space for every member's tasks and activities. You shouldn't have to put up with fishing tackle in the kitchen, any more than your husband should have to clear dress patterns off his desk. Teenagers with homework should be able to escape from adults' TV programs, and their parents shouldn't have to trip over baseball bats and electric guitars in the hall.

Ask yourself what your main problems are. Finding a place to entertain your husband's colleagues in a civilized way in a house cluttered with sports equipment, rock collections, and assorted fan magazines? Achieving smart, sophisticated surroundings on a tiny paycheck? Too many books and papers? A husband who's a ham radio fiend?

Sort out your problems and solutions in the early stages of planning. If one of the family needs a workroom, and will make the house a mess without it, give up some space somewhere so he can muck about in peace. If you have too many stacks of encyclopedias, old *National Geographics*, Monopoly boards, road maps, and whodunits, put up some shelves. Or buy some inexpensive storage units—the kind you can add to as your collection grows. Or reorganize a closet, install a good light in it, and put the less decorative part of the col-

lection in there away from general view.

Are you frightened by color schemes? Does your mind go blank at words like "monochromatic" and "complementary?" Relax! Choosing colors is one of the most pleasant parts of decorating, and less rule-bound than you may think. Be bold when choosing colors and fabrics. Choose colors because you like them and, in the case of other people's rooms, because *they* like them—not because certain colors are re-

commended for kitchens, or supposedly "go together," or are easy to clean. Fortunately, most shades can now be obtained in wash-able materials, and this applies to paint as well as fabrics. The marvelous thing about decorating is the variety of fabrics and materials available to express every con-ceivable taste and personality. Some houses are an absolute kaleidoscope of shapes, pat-terns, colors, and textures. If you can live in this kind of patchwork world, go ahead and

Right: this complementary color scheme uses vivid blue and yellow against restful cream colored walls. Notice the simple, effective window treatment. Another view of the same room is on page 65.

make the most of it. If deep colors are what excite you, choose one you like and carry it throughout the house: walls and carpeting, hallway and bathroom. This can give a splendid, bold effect. If you prefer more subdued surroundings, beige, cream, and even certain shades of gray are all excellent.

The difficulty with color is that it changes according to the kind and amount of natural or artificial light shining on it, according to the texture of the material itself, and according to the other colors placed near it. Without years of interior decorating experience—and even with—it's hard to choose a color from a small sample, because it will look different in bulk. It's usually safe to choose colors you often wear. Rely on your instincts, and don't try to be too intellectual about it. Rules are made to be broken.

You may find it helpful, however, to follow this general rule: it's usually best to choose one basic color for use in large amounts, one secondary color to contrast with the main color, and, if desired, one or more accent colors to be used in small splashes. The basic color can be anything from a neutral, such as beige, to deep blue or maroon. You can change the basic color from room to room, or carry out the same color balance throughout most of the house or apartment.

Another color idea is to use the secondary color of the living room as the basic color in the master bedroom. You may prefer to use completely different color schemes in different rooms. The olive green that you've featured in your spacious living room may be too somber for a small bedroom with a northern exposure. Also, you'll probably find that your children will want something different from anything you had in mind. Most children love the primary colors— red, blue, and yellow. The subtleties of cream and terra cotta leave them cold. If your child wants his room painted bright royal blue, you might try royal blue on one wall, and patterned paper on the others.

What if you make a mistake? It sometimes happens, even to experienced decorators. Don't be too proud to change your mind if you realize half-way through painting a wall that the shade you've chosen is all wrong. On the other hand, if you've given enough thought to color beforehand, this shouldn't happen. You can minimize the risk of color mistakes by painting a large piece of cardboard with the color of your choice, and holding it up in various parts of the room, in

Above: sunny yellow and apple green—an example of a related color scheme. For children's rooms, fairly intense colors are usually preferable, as compared with soft, subtle shades of the same hues.

Above: a monochromatic color scheme of blue with white. A lilac throw pillow provides an accent color. Varying the shades and intensities of the chosen hue will add interest to a monochromatic plan.

different lights. Try to look at the room objectively. Look at the basic shape of the room. Is there anything about it you would like to emphasize? Anything you want to hide? Is there an alcove you could make into an interesting feature? Are some walls being wasted? Don't forget the lighting—any wiring for new lights should be done before you start painting.

Big rooms call for big furniture, bold wallpaper patterns, curtains covering a whole wall. This may sound expensive, but some of the sheer fabrics look best with no lining, and can be easily made up at home. If you prefer solid color walls to patterned paper, use a few big pictures for dramatic impact, or cover a large part of one wall with a grouping of pictures—large, small, or mixed.

If your collection is of objects rather than paintings, cover a whole wall or more

There's no need to be intimidated by blank walls. With a little imagination—and surprisingly little money—you can make a room come alive like this one (right). The owners painted the walls off-white to make a neutral background for a group of reproductions of works by major modern artists. They mounted and framed the pictures themselves, and arranged them above a 9-foot long, wall-hung buffet of white painted pine. Drop-front sections of the buffet hold tableware and a bar. The illuminated center section displays some of the accessories, while others, placed along the top, lend more visual interest to the arrangement.

with a shelving system. Try plain shelving put onto movable brackets, which you can move around to accommodate any size and shape of thing you want to shelve: television, books, magazines, games, and records.

In making your decorating plans, stick to your own judgment. Choose colors, textures, furniture that *you* like (although, in the case of chairs, you should make sure that others can sit in them comfortably). Your friends don't want to see a replica of their own home when they come to visit you. They want to feel stimulated, comfortable, and relaxed. Comfort is the main criterion. What on earth is the use of an ultra-fashionable modern sofa if everyone who sits on it gets backache or cramp in the legs? Warmth, hospitality, and comfort are what a home is all about.

For example, use bunk beds in a children's room, by all means, but make sure the child

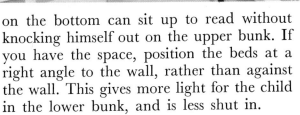

Left: a dull bathroom can be transformed into a beautiful one. Here, floral printed wallpaper is a pretty background, and shelves disguise an awkward recess, providing space for color coordinated towels, jars of bath salts, etc. Other charming touches: a picture, and a vase of flowers.

on the bottom can sit up to read without knocking himself out on the upper bunk. If you have the space, position the beds at a right angle to the wall, rather than against the wall. This gives more light for the child in the lower bunk, and is less shut in.

Aim to use all the rooms in your house to their fullest. A room that's used only for sleeping is wasted for half its life, and has a neglected feeling about it—no matter how neat and tidy it is. Your bedroom probably has enough extra space to include a small office or sewing area. You'll find it an ideal refuge—particularly when your children reach the party-giving teens—if you arrange it as a second sitting room, with all the comforts of armchairs, hi-fi, television, and books. A separate dining room may seem a wasted luxury unless you are giving frequent dinner parties. If you take your meals in the kitchen, why not use the dining room for other purposes? Convert it into a library, study, or guest room.

Whatever decorating plans you make will cost money, but if you are at all good with your hands, you can take some of the sting from the the cost by painting walls and furniture yourself, by doing your own wall-papering, and by making your own slip-

Don't be afraid to be bold in your use of color and pattern—unless, of course, you prefer muted colors. This kitchen owes a lot to the yellow and green wallpaper, the choice of appliances in a matching green, and floor and accessories in yellow. Cabinets painted white set off the other colors. Space under the stairs that would otherwise be wasted accommodates the washing machine nicely.

covers, curtains, and throw pillows. You will save money by learning something about fabrics, carpets, paints, and their uses. Some draperies don't need lining. Some walls are better painted instead of covered with an expensive wall covering. There are carpets for many different kinds of floor and many different kinds of wear, and sometimes a cheaper kind is ideal for the purpose. You'll also save money if you know how to convert existing furniture into something more modern or more useful, and if you know where to buy cheap unpainted furniture that you can paint or stain yourself.

You can make rugs and lampshades, put up your own shelving, lay some kinds of flooring yourself, scrape and wax or varnish tables, put up ceramic wall tiles. What you save by do-it-yourself you can spend on a leather chair, or an original painting.

Bear in mind that situations and people change. It is no longer necessary, or even a good idea, to buy everything to last forever. The home you arrange for two young adults and one toddler may be entirely wrong for two adults and three teenagers some years later. Aim for flexibility. Don't think you have to decorate the whole house at once. Sometimes it's better to use makeshift items until you can find, or afford, something that's exactly right.

Before making any final decisions, look around locally to see what's available. Don't rush out and buy right away. Look at your friends' homes. Don't steal their ideas, but don't be too proud to adapt some of them to your own environment.

Look through magazines, in shop windows, home furnishings exhibits, museums. Use any opportunity to consider something

new. The whole point of this book is that you needn't spend a fortune to create a home with character, comfort, and charm. You will, however, need a good deal of thought, patience, energy, enthusiasm, and courage. The more you are willing to do things yourself, the less you will need to spend.

The book has been organized in terms of materials, and not into different kinds of rooms, for the traditional ideas on appropriate materials for different rooms are changing. There is no reason nowadays why you shouldn't have carpet in the kitchen, wallpaper in the bathroom, and ceramic tiles in the living room. All you need is some understanding of the special characteristics of the various materials, and the correct way to handle them. Once you have this knowledge, you can let your imagination be your guide to a beautiful home.

Personal touches make the difference between a room that is merely tastefully furnished and one that expresses the personalities of those who live there. Left: a room for someone who likes old-fashioned charm. The simple lines of the bed and desk are complemented by the richly figured Victorian screen.

Above: a "find" from some market or antique shop makes a beautiful ornament for a living room wall. The colors in the frame are picked up in the scatter cushions.

Left: keep your mind open to various uses for accessories you have, and for those you see in the shops. This colorful pot was probably intended for a plant, but it makes a suitable and attractive container for magazines.

Right: there's no reason why furnishings can't be amusing as well as useful. Some clever carpentry created this group of geese for a coat rack.

Ways With Walls
2

Decorating conventions— like most conventions— are made to be broken. If you think walls must be painted a solid color, think again. This children's room was turned into a charming fantasy world with a storybook mural. If you can't paint yourself, you can always use a wallpaper mural.

Walls are the background against which you live your life. What you do with them can alter the whole feel of the house, and they therefore deserve a good deal of attention in the planning stages, and a first-class job when it comes to doing them.

First, take a good look at the areas in your home. Decide which shapes you want to emphasize, which to camouflage. For example, if a room has an awkward corner jutting out, or a peculiar looking recess, consider covering the walls with wallpaper of a small pattern. The design of the paper will attract attention to itself, making the irregularities of the wall less obvious.

On the other hand, if you have an alcove or some other interesting wall feature, you can emphasize it by papering it in a pattern, and painting the rest of the room in a solid color harmonizing with the paper. If there is an attractive archway between your living and dining rooms, paint one room in a dramatically contrasting color to emphasize the shape of the arch. Highlight any attractive moldings on the ceiling or around doors and windows by painting them in a color contrasting with the rest of the wall. To accentuate the paneling on a door, use a contrasting shade of paint on the panels. If a room is long and narrow, paint one of the end walls an intense color, or paper it with a bold pattern, or panel it with dark wood. This kind of treatment will give the illusion of bringing the end wall forward, counteracting the long, narrow effect.

You needn't plan to do all the walls in your house at one fell swoop, but you should plan all of them together, with a view toward the relationships between adjoining rooms.

You may want to give a hallway a color scheme of its own, but make sure that the scheme is in keeping with the rooms into which the hall leads.

Bear in mind that pale colors and smooth surfaces will give a serene effect. Purples, deep browns, black, and midnight blue are positive colors, and will emphasize the wall areas in the room. These colors won't overwhelm the room if you paint ceilings and woodwork white or off-white, and select furniture that can hold its own with the wall color. To make a room look larger, use a light color on the walls. To make a dark room brighter, use a warm color, such as yellow or orange, or use lots of white with bright accents of other colors. Wood paneling gives a special warmth to a room. Remember, in choosing any color—but particularly the color for your walls—that a color will look brighter in a large area than it does in a small sample; so choose a color slightly lighter or duller than you want the walls to look.

If you already have your carpet, and some or all of your furniture, take some color samples to the paint or wall covering shop. Take a fairly large piece of fabric or carpet, if possible. Better still, bring the paint or paper samples home, and look at them in the room, against your existing decor. Look at the colors in both natural and artificial light. Don't worry about matching shades exactly; a slight variation in shade from one material to another is inevitable and, in fact, adds interest to the room.

While you are considering the color for your walls, keep in mind the various patterns and textures available. The possibilities are

more varied than you may think. In addition to paint and wallpaper, you have a choice of cloth coverings; tiles, including ceramic, cork, and synthetics; paneling; and brick. You can even buy a paint that will create a stucco effect—but make sure before you apply it that this is what you will want for ever and ever.

Your selection of wall covering will be determined not only by the effect you wish to create, but also by the cost, durability, and washability of the material. Fortunately, many, if not most, paints and wall coverings are easy to keep clean.

Paint. If you decide on paint, you still face the choice of which kind. Your paint or hardware store will carry several kinds of paints, varnishes, and enamels. For decorating large areas, it is advisable to choose one of only two basic types: water soluble (latex and acrylic), and solvent soluble (oil and alkyd). Alkyd paint doesn't flow as well or cover as easily as oil paint, and you still have to use turpentine or a special solvent to thin it as well as to clean up. Water soluble paints are recommended for beginners, because they have several practical advantages: they dry fast; they don't show lap or brush marks; they have little, if any, smell; spatters of paint can be wiped up with a damp cloth; brushes and rollers can be cleaned with soap and water; *you* can be cleaned with soap and water.

Originally, water soluble paints came only in flat finishes, but semi-gloss is now available. Gloss and semi-gloss paints are practical for kitchens, bathrooms, and woodwork, because grease, soot, and oily fingerprints wash off better. On the other hand, gloss paint tends to give off a glare, which you may find disagreeable.

When buying paint, the first rule is: buy enough. You can always use any extra paint for touch ups, whereas, if you run short before the job is finished, you'll have the impossible task of trying to match up the original batch of paint. The same applies to wallpaper. Buy an extra roll to guard against the possibility of needing more paper when

Above: this dramatic red and black color scheme gets most of its impact from the walls, covered in rich red fabric with black trim. Simple furnishings, and a white ceiling with black beams, relieve the intensity of the large areas of red.
Right: a high ceiling was "lowered" by painting the ceiling and upper part of the walls a mustard yellow, and defining the joining of the two colors with a narrow band of red.

Above: you can use paint to emphasize architectural features. White paint highlights the graceful line of the arch (above) and makes a frame for the built-in bookshelves. An entrance hall (left) gains depth and drama with contrasting wall colors. Below and right: dark walls are a good foil for bright colored furnishings and white curtains.

Color Basics

Below: This color wheel shows the primary colors (red, blue, and yellow) ; the secondary colors (violet, orange, green), which are composed of equal parts of adjacent primary colors ; and intermediate colors lying between the primary and secondary colors. The inner and outer sections show shades and tints of the colors, formed by mixing them with black and white.

Opposite: The three basic types of color scheme are illustrated in these three drawings. A monochromatic scheme uses one color, in various tints and shades and varying degrees of intensity. A related color scheme uses colors that lie adjacent to each other on the color wheel, often including their tints, shades, and intermediate hues. A complementary scheme uses colors that lie opposite each other (or nearly opposite) on the wheel. Remember that colors affect each other. The squares at far right show how the same color, red-orange, changes slightly when surrounded by yellow-green, blue, and lilac.

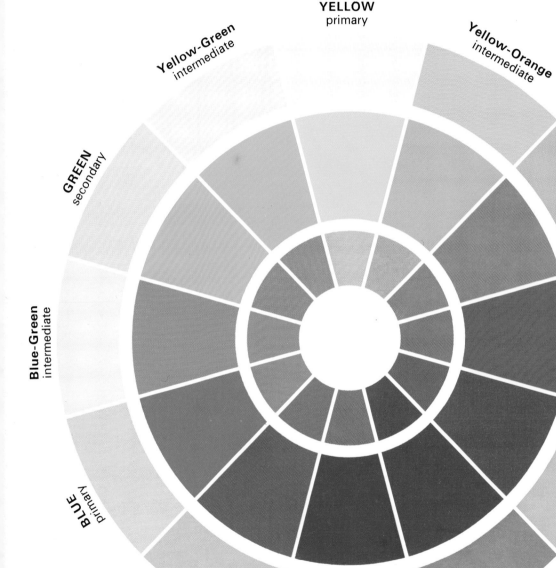

An example of a monochromatic color scheme.

An example of a related color scheme.

An example of a complementary color scheme.

31

the dealer's sold the last of that pattern.

How much is enough? You must measure the room carefully, including the insides of closets. Measure the height and width of each wall, and multiply to get the square feet for that wall. Add up the measurements for the walls and closet interiors to get the total area. Similarly, measure the window areas, and subtract that total from your wall area. The paint can will specify the number of square feet the contents will cover. Remember to buy some extra to be on the safe side.

When you buy your paint, always have the store put it on their shaking machine. This mechanical stirring mixes paint well, and saves you time and bother. If you don't have this done, or have delayed painting for several days, turn the cans over the day

Above: striking bamboo patterned wallpaper was used here to set a tropical mood for the furnishings. The strong pattern also serves to distract attention from several jogs in the room's construction.

Left: the really exciting possibilities of wallpaper are suggested in this beautiful bathroom. Not a job for a novice paperhanger, but it might be worth paying a professional to cover this small area.

Right: matching wallpaper and fabric are used with good effect in this green and white room. The Oriental-look pattern enlivens the far wall, while plain green around the fireplace gives the eye a rest, and provides a background for the picture.

Below: a room for someone who likes Mondrian: red-and-white lattice printed fabric covers one wall and the bed in a pleasing rectangular design.

before you do the job. You will then only have to give the paint an extra stir with a stick, or with the paint stirrer of an electric drill.

Before you actually begin work, it's a good idea to check the color on a large surface. Buy a showcard (28 inches by 44 inches) from an art supply store, and paint this first. Allow it to dry, then hold it against the wall for an accurate indication of how the color will look when applied to the wall. If the color is wrong, you can have it corrected at the paint store.

In addition to the paint, you'll need a brush, roller, or foam pad for applying it. For the amateur decorator, a paintbrush can be a tricky implement. Brush marks, drips, and streaks are difficult to prevent. You'll be wise if you stick to other kinds of applicators, such as rollers—which now come in sizes to handle all jobs—bristleless polyfoam brushes (disposable), and pads. If you compare spreading power, all of these newer applicators give faster and better results than do brushes—at least for the amateur. Besides, rollers, pads, and the polyfoam brushes are relatively inexpensive.

You can purchase rollers of many different types of fiber and length of nap to give you the kind of coverage you need. Medium nap synthetic lamb's wool is the cover most often used for painting flat latex or alkyd paints on walls or ceilings. Use short nap mohair covers for a smooth job with glossy or semi-gloss enamels. Deep nap rollers are specifically designed for use on rough surfaces, such as concrete, cinder block, brickwork, or stucco.

For painting narrow areas, as well as for use on flat trim and moldings, there are rollers that measure only three inches in width. There are also doughnut-shaped rollers, called corner rollers, to reach all the way into corners when both surfaces will be painted the same color.

As you can see, painting has become much easier for the amateur; and when you think of the money you'll save by doing it yourself, you shouldn't hesitate to tackle the job. Your paint dealer can give you further advice in selecting materials.

Wallpaper. Wonderful decorating possibilities open up if you consider wallpaper—either for an entire room, or as an accent for one wall or a small area. For example, if you plan to have a system of open shelves along one wall, you could make this wall even more interesting by covering it first with wallpaper in a small- to medium-sized pattern. This will give additional drama to the wall, and keep it from looking like everyone else's shelf system. Liven up an antiseptic looking tiled bathroom with a splash of daisies or poppies around the mirror. Use wallpaper in small, dull areas— such as the space under a stairway. With the right kind of lighting to show off the pattern, you've converted a dead spot into a visual surprise. This, incidentally, is part of the secret of successful decorating—balancing elements that relax with elements that excite. Interesting wallpaper patterns are an excellent way to do this.

A word of warning, however. Don't overdo patterns in your decorating scheme. One pattern is generally enough for a room, so if you have figured paper on the walls, you should probably restrict yourself to solids in your carpet, draperies, and furniture. Like all rules, though, this one has exceptions. You can easily combine a tone-on-tone carpet, or even a striped chair seat, with your figured paper. Professional decorators often put two patterns in one room— provided that the patterns complement each other, instead of competing. A small allover pattern will often live happily with a large

Brick is beautiful; and if you're lucky enough to have brick interior walls, make the most of them. Natural red brick (left) heightens the warm tones of the furnishings. Whitewashed brick (below left) provides a textured contrast for an oak chair and shelves. Below: an opulent look was achieved in this bathroom with the use of a marble-finish laminate wall covering to harmonize with the marble wash basin.

Above: warm wood paneled walls help to make this dining area inviting. The golden brown tones of the wood are complemented by crisp blue and white. Below: this arresting wall treatment was created by hanging a collection of blue plates in a seemingly random pattern, and visually echoing their designs with motifs painted on the wall. Notice how the door has been integrated into the scheme.

floral print, for example. Combining two patterns successfully takes skill and an experienced eye, however. Bear in mind when selecting wallpaper that your fabric choices will be somewhat restricted by it.

As for the practical aspects of papering, they're a bit more difficult than for painting. You must, of course, hang the paper absolutely vertically, and this doesn't always follow the line of the walls; you must match the pattern from one strip to the next; and you must do this with material that is wet, sticky, and rather heavy—sometimes while you are standing on a stepladder. Still, you can take courage from the fact that some of the techniques have been simplified. One of the great boons for the do-it-yourself decorator is prepasted papers. You still have to wet the paper, of course, but the pasting has been done for you, and this cuts down on time and trouble. You also have a choice of papers that come with an adhesive backing. All you have to do is peel off the backing, and stick on the paper—no wetting needed.

If you're considering wallpaper, have a look through the samples at your dealer's. He'll probably let you take some books home for leisurely inspection.

Other wall coverings. Wallpaper is just the beginning, for today you have a wide choice of applied wall coverings—many of them much more suitable than paint or wallpaper for walls that are rough or cracked. Vinyls are big decorating news. Easily washed, they are especially appropriate in kitchen, bathroom, and children's room. Fabric wall coverings give visual warmth and interesting texture as well. Some burlaps, and other fabrics, have a special backing that makes them easier to hang. As a beginner, beware of hanging anything that might stretch, such as felt.

There's another way to use fabric on a wall, and that is by covering a whole wall with floor-length draperies. Expensive? Not if you use inexpensive fabric. Burlap, for example, comes in lovely colors, and so do many other inexpensive cottons and syn-

thetics. Or use colored or printed sheets. The soft folds of the draperies give an intimate, cozy feeling to a room. This is an especially good way to give a room a face lift if you don't need to repaint or repaper, but are bored with the walls as they are.

Ceramic tiles are among the most exciting, effective, and practical of wall coverings. Don't restrict their use to the bathroom. Modern style rooms — particularly those including shaggy rugs and nubby-textured fabrics—gain more excitement through skillful use of ceramic tiles. These tiles are apt to be expensive, but, fortunately, you can get a big effect with a small tiled area. Put them around your fireplace, or between two windows, or above a headboardless bed.

Cork and vinyl wall tiles are easier to apply; many come with adhesive backing. Cork is a good choice for one wall of a playroom, because it tends to absorb sound, and can be used as a bulletin board. Dark brown cork makes a handsome background for a study.

If you love the rich look of wood paneling, you'll be glad to know that you have a choice of many types of panels, some of them adhesive-backed for easy installation. Of course, paneling is more expensive than paint or wallpaper, but if used on one wall only, with the rest of the room painted or papered, it can be even more effective than if used all over.

You can also buy various kinds of moldings to attach to the walls. These are useful not only for hanging pictures, but also for creating architectural interest in a room. You can attach a chair rail in your dining room, give a window a handsome frame, or lower a ceiling by putting a strip of molding partway down, and painting the upper part of the walls to match the ceiling.

As you can see, the walls of your home are not just neutral areas, but potentially an important part of your decorating scheme. Use your imagination to create a background that will enhance your furnishings, and give a welcome feeling to each room that you have in your home.

Above: the hard-edge Art Deco style, popular in the 1920's, is enjoying a revival. In this bathroom, cork tiles have been cut and arranged in an Art Deco design.

Right: a more traditional look using cork tiles in a bathroom. The warm tones of the cork, the frame of the mirror, and the flowers all help to make the room attractive.

Above: a clever use of mirror tiles. Set at different heights among the ceramic tiles, they make it easy for children to learn grooming habits. A larger mirror for adults is hung above them.
Left: blue and white patterned ceramic tiles are used here for a kitchen anyone would enjoy working in. Shutters make a pretty window treatment.

37

Floor Planning

3

Choosing a floor covering is a bit more complex than selecting a treatment for your walls. Besides considering appearance and cost, you must also give some thought to wear and tear, soil and spills. Also, floor coverings are more expensive than most coverings—and certainly more expensive than paint—and so they must last longer. You need to make sure that you'll be happy with your choice for a number of years.

As a general rule, you should plan your floors and walls at the same time, so that you have a picture in your mind of how they will complement each other in color and texture. If you plan to have walls and floors the same, or nearly the same, color, you should buy your floor covering first, because it is much easier to have paint mixed to the desired shade than to find the right color of carpet or tiles to go with already painted walls.

Your first step in deciding on floor coverings should be to make a careful evaluation of your requirements. Here are some of the questions you should consider:

1. What kind of floor does the room already have? Most floors, except for bathroom, kitchen, and basement, are hardwood. This kind of floor can be beautiful if well sanded and well maintained, but most people prefer to cover them—either partially or entirely—with wall-to-wall carpeting, rugs, or some other material that will give warmth, and be easier to maintain than the natural flooring. If you're lucky enough to have

parquet wood floors, you'll probably want to show them off by using small area rugs. Similarly, if you have a stone or brick floor, you can make it a featured attraction of the room, adding only a shaggy rug or some straw matting for a cozy touch. If you live in an old house whose floors are in bad condition, room-size rugs or wall-to-wall carpeting will conceal them nicely.

2. What is the room used for? This is the most important factor in determining the general type of floor covering you'll want. For example, in the kitchen you'll need something that is easy to clean, and that will also take a lot of wear. You'll want something that is comfortable underfoot. The most satisfactory covering for your needs may be linoleum, vinyl, or vinyl tiles, which come in a wide range of colors and designs. Cushioned vinyl has a spongy backing, which makes for extra comfort for the feet. Consider, also, the possibility of carpeting your kitchen. It's not as wild as it sounds. Some kinds of carpet—such as nylon—are easily cleaned, and unless you have very small children constantly grinding cookie crumbs and peanut butter underfoot, you may find carpeting not only comfortable, but also attractive.

Unlike the kitchen, bedroom floors generally get very little wear, except for children's rooms. Here, you'll probably want something soft—if not wall-to-wall carpeting, at least a scatter rug for beside the bed. You can economize a bit on durability in a bedroom rug, because bedrooms get much less traffic than living and dining rooms.

In a child's bedroom, you may want to divide the floor into two areas, covering one part with a soft rug so that the child can

Wall-to-wall carpeting is warm and comfortable, but it can be expensive. Carpet tiles make an economical substitute. You can lay them yourself, and move them to a new home when the time comes.

The choice of a flooring depends a great deal on the use of the room that it's to go in. For a children's room (above), these bright gold-and-white vinyl tiles provide a hard wearing, easy-care surface. The pretty, deep pile carpeting (right) is well-suited to a room that gets only light traffic.

sprawl on the floor comfortably, and the other area with something smooth, such as linoleum, that will provide a good surface for building blocks and other toys.

In the dining room you'll need something fairly hard wearing, and preferably easy to clean. Either vinyl tiles, or a rug in a medium shade or busy pattern, or carpet tiles, would be good.

Most people prefer carpeting or a room-size rug for the living room. A rug has practical advantages over a carpet in that no installation is required, and it can be sent out for cleaning, whereas a carpet must be cleaned in the home.

Most bathrooms already have a ceramic tile floor, and people generally add only a bathmat and a small rug in front of the basin. If you have a taste for luxury, cover the bathroom floor in inexpensive nylon carpeting. You can buy a length of rubber-backed carpet in a choice of many colors, and cut it to fit around your bathroom fixtures.

3. Is sound absorbency important? Some apartment leases stipulate that a certain amount of the floor area must be covered by rugs. This is mainly to make the apartment more soundproof for the sake of other tenants. Even if you live in a house of your own, you may give high priority to cutting down noise, and want to cover most of your floors with soft material.

4. Is temperature an important factor? If you live in a cold climate, you may need carpeting or room-size rugs throughout most of your home, because they do a lot to keep a room warm. If you live in a hot climate, you may prefer the cooler look and feel of tiles (ceramic or vinyl), and straw matting.

5. Is cleanability of primary importance? With pets or small children, you'll be smart to choose floor coverings that can be easily

cleaned, such as nylon carpeting or vinyl.
6. How long do you expect to remain in your
present home? In a mobile society such as
ours, it's hard to say. Your husband may be
transferred several times by his company
before you can settle down more or less
permanently. A growing family may require
a move to larger quarters. So, before you
invest in wall-to-wall carpeting, give some
serious thought to your chances of getting
long-term use from it.

While weighing all these practical matters,
you'll also be thinking about the kind of
look you want for each room. A floor
covering may not be the most striking object
in a room—although it *can* be—but it does
play an important part in establishing a
"feeling" for a room. Wall-to-wall carpet
will make a room look larger, and give a
feeling of continuity from one room to the
next. An area rug can unify a furniture
grouping, giving a feeling of intimacy to that
part of the room. A shaggy rug will give a
feeling of warmth and coziness. Terra cotta
tiles give a Mediterranean flavor to a room;
straw matting, an informal look, reminiscent

41

of the South Seas. Consider the textures and patterns you'll want to have in the room—or those you already have. If, for example, you plan to use a busy patterned wallpaper, you should probably avoid shaggy rugs or patterned tiles. The rule of thumb for both patterns and textures is: contrast. Put rough textures next to smooth; set off interesting patterns with relaxing plain colors.

Once you decide on the general type of floor covering you want for each room, you're faced with the business of choosing specific products. Buying carpeting is one of

made on a broad loom. It comes in widths of 9, 12, and 15 feet, and is sold by the square yard. (Occasionally the price quoted is for the square foot—1/9th the area of a square yard.) Often the price includes padding and installation.

To get the amount of carpeting you need for a room, you often have wastage. Depending on the size and shape of the room, this can cost a fair amount of money. For example, if your room is 13 feet wide, you will need to buy the 15 foot width, and will have a strip 2 feet wide left over. If the room

Left: area rugs enhance traditional furnishings. This one, in yellow and magenta, repeats the shape of the area between bed and wall, and complements the floor. (For another example of an area rug, see the top of page 63.)

Right: traditional styles can also live happily with wall-to-wall carpeting, even when it's an informal, shaggy type. Notice how the glass coffee table permits more of the carpet to be seen, giving a spacious look to the room.

the most pitfall-strewn shopping ventures you can undertake. Unless you can afford to spend a great deal of money, you will need to shop around very carefully, and you will encounter many false "bargains" in your search. Here are a few things you should know before you start shopping.

First of all—the term "broadloom." This has nothing to do with the quality or type of carpet; it simply means that the carpet was

is 21 feet long, you have a leftover strip equal to $4\frac{2}{3}$ square yards. If the carpet costs $10 a square yard, this represents just under $50 wasted. You can use the extra carpeting by cutting it into small pieces to lay over much used areas. If you'd rather avoid the wastage, however, you can buy the 12-foot width and have a narrow strip seamed onto it in a place that won't show much.

Differences in the quality of the fibers

themselves can be subtle and difficult for the layman to distinguish, but you can easily compare differences in *density*—and this has a lot to do with the looks and durability of the carpet. Bend the sample backward to see how much of the backing shows through. The shorter the pile of the carpet, the denser it should be. A shaggy rug can be much less dense than a velvet type, because the fibers overlap to create the effect of density.

Another important aspect of a carpet's construction is whether it is woven or tufted. Other things being equal, a woven rug is more durable than one in which the fibers are tufted—that is, individually sewn onto the backing. However, a dense tufted carpet, if it has a double backing, can give satisfactory wear.

The various fibers and construction methods can be used to produce several different

These two charts will help you evaluate the various kinds of carpets and rugs you find in the stores. In examining a carpet, look for density—a very important factor (less important in shag types).

Carpet Textures

Velvet (also known as Plush, Frieze, and Splush)
Has an even, generally dense pile; resists crushing and bending; tends to show footprints, which is desirable for shadowing (takes away from the "flat look"). This type of carpet tends to show soil more than others; not the best for stair covering.

Shag
Comes in varying yarn lengths (up to two inches); gives grass-like appearance. Used for both formal and informal settings; does not wear well on stairs. Look for dyed back, which camouflages wear.

Velvet Shag
A high, soft pile that easily shows indentations from traffic; tends to mat in high traffic areas.

Random Sheared
A mixture of loops and cut pile with a sculptured effect; if pile is not thick, pattern may flatten out; excellent for high-traffic areas; wears well on stairs.

Tip-Sheared
Also a mixture of loops and cut pile, but with a one-level surface.

One-Level Looped
Tightly woven looped carpet; very strong; withstands water and stains; wears well on stairs.

Two-Level Looped or "Sculptured"
Has a sculptured effect; very durable; wears well on stairs.

kinds of textures. The chart opposite shows some of these textures, and points out the main characteristics of each. One texture does not necessarily wear better than another of comparable quality; however, some will retain their good looks better than others. Novelty weaves, such as shag, may mat rather badly in heavy traffic areas.

Good padding is essential for a rug or carpeting. It will absorb wear to prolong the life of the carpet, besides giving extra warmth and comfort. You have a choice of several different kinds of padding: polyurethane, sponge rubber, and hair-and-jute mixtures. The first two have excellent resiliency, but the less expensive hair-and-jute is generally satisfactory.

When selecting carpeting, be sure to look at the carpet sample on the floor, not just on a vertical rack. Look at it in daylight as well as in artificial light. If possible, take a sample home with you to look at against other colors in the room. If not, bring your fabric swatches with you to the store. Carpet colors tend to gray with time and wear, so it's a good idea to buy a color slightly more intense than you want. When you have made your selection, ask for a sample of both carpet and padding to take home so that you can compare it with what is delivered.

Of course, you'll be wise if you wait for carpet sales, usually held twice a year by department stores. You can also get bargains at the rug specialty stores and rug warehouses in the larger cities. It's sometimes possible to buy carpeting at greatly reduced prices if part of it is defective. You may be able to cut away the defective part, or hide it under a piece of furniture.

Carpet Fibers

FIBER	PLUS QUALITIES	MINUS QUALITIES	CLEANABILITY
Wool	Excellent durability; springy and crush-resistant; adaptable to styling; flame resistant.	Must be mothproofed; can be damaged by alkaline detergents; waste or reprocessed wool is a poor choice.	Needs cleaning less frequently than synthetics, but is more difficult to clean.
Acrylic *Trade names:* Acrilan, Creslan, Orlon, Sayelle, Zefran, Zefkrome.	Takes color well; springy and crush-resistant; good soil resistance; resists mildew and sun.	Not very fire resistant; generates static electricity; may pill.	Cleans very well.
Modacrylics *Trade names:* Verel, Dynel, Elura	Used in blends for flame resistance; very durable; usable in high-pile rugs.	Lacks good resilience; pills and shreds easily.	Cleans very well.
Nylon *Trade names:* Anso, Antron, Cadon, Caprolan, Cumuloft, Enkalure, Enkaloft	Exceptional durability; springy and crush resistant; nonallergenic; not affected by mildew.	Soils easily in bright colors; pills in staple loop pile; some static electricity; fiber melts; cool to touch; buy virgin, not waste, nylon.	Excellent.
Polyester *Trade names:* Avlin, Dacron, Fortrel, Encron, Kodel, Trevira	Excellent durability and crush resistance; not affected by moths or mildew.	Cool to touch; some pilling and static electricity.	Excellent.
Olefin *Trade names:* Vectra, Herculon, Marvess, Polycrest	Good durability; good soil resistance; nonallergenic, lightweight.	Fiber melts in lower grades; likely to crush.	When stains set in, they are difficult to remove.
Polypropylene	Very good wearing; good resistance to crushing and soiling; outstanding resistance to stains.	Poor flame resistance; crushes easily; soils fairly easily.	Excellent.
Cotton	Soft; excellent durability; not subject to moths or mildew.	Fiber and color can be destroyed by lye or bleach.	Small rugs can be machine washed, carpet shampooed successfully.
Rayon	Takes color well; is soft; good chemical resistance; not affected by moths.	In less dense pile, has poor flame resistance; crushes; poor durability and soil resistance.	As cleanable as cotton.
Polyester pneumacel From DuPont Labs and Simmons Corp.	Nonflammable, odorless, nonallergenic, mold and mildew resistant. Will not pack, form craters, or loose plumpness; firm and resilient.	This is a relatively new fiber and has not been found deficient in quality.	

Left: a Mediterranean flavor has been given to this stairway with Spanish ceramic tiles on the stair risers. The picture shows the possibility of making a hallway into an attractive and interesting "room" in its own right, rather than just a link between other rooms.

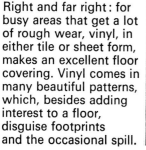

Right and far right: for busy areas that get a lot of rough wear, vinyl, in either tile or sheet form, makes an excellent floor covering. Vinyl comes in many beautiful patterns, which, besides adding interest to a floor, disguise footprints and the occasional spill.

Rugs have the advantage over carpeting in that they can be moved from one house—or room—to another, and they can be turned to distribute wear. You also save the installation charges. However, unless the rug covers all but a few inches of the floor, you may need to have the floors sanded and polished, which is expensive to have done, and hard to do yourself.

A rug with an interesting design is not just a background to your furnishings, but also a decorative feature in itself. With simple furnishings, such a rug is especially effective. The most prized of all are Oriental rugs, which lend drama to both modern and traditional interiors. Although these are often extremely expensive, it is possible to find bargains among secondhand Oriental rugs.

One advantage of area rugs is that you can, with a little patience, make them yourself—thereby saving some money while adding your own creative touch to your home. Braided rugs are easy to make, and are well suited to Early American, and some modern, interiors. Use scraps of leftover fabric, or pick up remnants at a fabric shop. Hooked rugs are also fun to make. You can buy kits containing yarn and patterned backing for both velvet pile and shaggy rya rugs. Or, you can buy plain backing and

Even so, if you're planning to stay in your present home for some time, you might invest in one of these handsome floorings, even if it's just for a small entrance hall.

Synthetic hard-surface floorings are much cheaper, and today you can choose among materials in a dazzling array of colors, patterns, and textures. Vinyl is the most popular. It comes in sheet form, and also in tiles, which you can put down yourself.

Vinyl tiles are easy to clean, extremely tough, and available in an enormous range of patterns and colors. The more complicated the design you have planned, the more careful you must be with the measuring and laying. You will find thin vinyl easy to cut, but it should be laid only in places where it won't get too much wear. Thick tiles are hard to cut, but last for years. Cheaper than solid vinyl tile is vinyl asbestos tile. It wears well and is stain resistant. Some vinyl asbestos tiles have an adhesive backing, so all you do is peel off the protective covering, and press the tile into place. Asphalt tile is the cheapest tile available, but it is not too much of a bargain because it tends to crack and dent, and requires a lot of cleaning and waxing.

Other popular hard-surface floorings are sheet vinyl and linoleum. Sheet flooring has the advantage over tiles in that it has no cracks in which dirt can accumulate (unless you have to seam it to cover a large area), and it tends to be slightly cheaper than tiles.

One thing to remember is that some sheet flooring, and some tiles, should not be used on or below ground level, because they are susceptible to damage from moisture. Check with your dealer before buying sheet flooring for these levels.

Tiles have the advantage of giving you the chance to design your own floor. You can create any number of interesting patterns by combining tiles of different colors, adding decorative strips, laying tiles on the diagonal, and alternating patterned with solid tiles. You also have the practical advantage of being able to replace a single damaged tile without disturbing the rest of the floor. (Be sure to buy extra tiles for this purpose.)

make up your own design as you want it.

Woven straw matting is an attractive covering suitable for a room that doesn't get a great deal of traffic. It's cheap and fairly sound absorbing, but tends to collect dust underneath, is difficult to clean, and needs dampening from time to time to prevent curling at the edges.

Among hard-surface floorings, you have a huge selection. The natural materials—such as brick, flagstone, marble, ceramic tiles, and terra cotta tiles—are not necessarily expensive in themselves, compared to carpeting, but must be installed professionally, which can add considerably to the cost.

The Well-dressed Window

4

A window treatment should do one or more things: provide an appropriate frame for a pleasant view; give privacy, when needed, for inhabitants; and contribute to the decorative scheme. The simple roller blind, left, frames the kitchen view of a pretty garden. Above, a Danish kitchen window was given an interesting design with a red checked gingham shade, net curtains, and a decorative set of scales.

Unless your house overlooks a huge rubbish dump or a dark alley, one of the most pleasant places to sit is by a window. Sunlight and a pretty view go a long way toward making a room attractive. If you've actually planned your house from the pile of bricks stage, you'll be able to have windows placed where you want them. Most of us, however, have to make the best of the windows we already have, emphasizing the attractive ones, and transforming the ones that are nondescript or awkwardly placed. Even a window without a pretty view can be a decorative feature of the room if it's treated with imagination.

You can divide windows roughly into three groups:

1. *Modern windows* are usually made with large areas of glass in simple frames, and are designed to let in the outdoors—visually, at least. They are often called picture windows. Some of them are more like a large glass wall—less an architectural feature of the room than a means of expanding the room to include the outdoors. In most cases, you'll need to cover the windows at least some of the time—for privacy or for warmth. In general, the best approach is a simple treatment. Plain, floor-length draperies are effective. If you buy ready-made ones or—better still—make them yourself, you needn't spend stacks of money on them. If you don't need the privacy and insulation of opaque draperies, cover the window with sheer curtains. Interesting weaves and colors in sheer fabrics make this an attractive type of window treatment. Light filters through the cloth to create beautiful effects. Even plain burlap, left unlined, will make a lovely

Right: a window above a street of handsome townhouses was given a gardenlike screen with window boxes, filled with a variety of plants, including string beans. It leaves a view of the street, while affording some daytime privacy for the occupants. Curtains give extra privacy.

window curtain at low cost. It comes in vivid colors that look especially cheerful with the sun shining through.

In choosing draperies for large areas, it's wise to avoid big splashy prints. Ninety-six square feet of cabbage roses could be rather overpowering. Small prints are safer, or choose a solid color among the many interesting textures available, from formal brocades to nubby homespuns.

Valances and cornices are best avoided on picture windows, because they tend to look heavy and out-of-proportion. Use a simple, modern curtain rod that doesn't show, such as a traverse rod, or an old-fashioned rod with big rings.

Although draw draperies and curtains are the most popular way of decorating picture windows, you needn't feel that this is the only way to treat them. If the view isn't particularly good, or if the window is too close to the street or to a neighbor's window —making you feel like goldfish—you may want something that will screen the view, without cutting out the sunlight. One good solution is to put up shelves, and fill them with plants. Few things do so much as plants to make a room inviting, and a profusion of them—in various shades and shapes—arranged attractively on shelves would make a beautiful "picture" for your picture window. A Venetian blind or shade hung behind the plants will provide total privacy when you want it.

Fretwork panels of wood, aluminum, or plastic, can be placed in front of the window. They will let in some light, and, at the same time, add interesting texture and design to the room.

50

Above: another kind of garden-window uses shelves attached to brackets in the window frame. The different varieties of plants add to the charm of the window.

Right: if your talent lies more in painting plants than in growing them, adorn a window or a glass door with a profusion of blossoms, as done in this modern foyer.

2. *Traditional windows*, found in Colonial style or Victorian houses, lend themselves to a variety of treatments. Some of them are decorative in themselves, with pretty small panes, and attractive molding. Floor-length draperies are the traditional way of treating these windows, but within this category, you still have many variations from which to choose: two straight panels, tie-backs, draw draperies, pleated valance, draped valance, cornice, concealed rod, visible rod with rings. You also have the option of adding glass curtains under the draperies, or a window

shade or blind for both looks and privacy.

The narrower draperies used on traditional windows allow you more scope in choosing prints. A boldly patterned fabric, distributed over several windows, can be very effective. Make sure, though, that the draperies don't unbalance the room visually. For example, if you have two windows in the same wall hung with dramatic looking draperies, you should have a balancing element elsewhere in the room. A large chair or sofa covered with the drapery fabric is one good solution. A "picture wall", or a large screen with an eye-catching design, are other possibilities.

For an informal look for traditional windows, use café curtains or short ruffled tie-backs. If the windows have attractive molding—and particularly if they're deep set windows—consider installing louvered shut-ters, painted to match the rest of the wood-work. This gives a sophisticated look to a room. Shutters are relatively expensive, so it's best to invest in them only if you plan to remain in the house for some years.

Less expensive ways of showing off handsome windows: roll-up shades or Venetian blinds. Roll-up shades are now available in a wonderful range of colors and designs. If you don't find what you want in the stores, you can trim your own, either with bands of colored tape, or with a design you paint or stencil on, or with fabric cut to the same size and glued on. (Use thin, closely woven fabric.) Venetian blinds needn't be boring. Now they come in pleasing colors, and some have narrow slats for a subtler effect. Blinds matching the woodwork or wall color will complement both modern and period decors.

52

Left: in a small room, windows can become the main decorative feature. This young couple trimmed their dining alcove window with a pretty printed roller shade, then doubled the effect with a mirror. Accessories decorate windowsill.

Right: vertical blinds are a good way to hide an unattractive view and give plenty of privacy, while affording good, diffused natural light. The blinds are available in a range of colors.

Below: many windows need two kinds of trimmings: one letting in some light, and another giving maximum privacy. This charming room features a decorative shade in a print to match the wallpaper, and a lace curtain to let in sunlight.

This is a good idea if you're just starting to decorate your home, because they'll provide privacy and good looks at relatively little cost. Later, if you like, you can add draperies. If you already have some white Venetian blinds, give them a new look by painting them, or changing to new decorative tapes.

If you like the opulent turn-of-the-century look, trim some windows with Austrian shades. You can even make your own, using special tapes and cords to sew on the back of the shades. One advantage to making your own is that you have a wide choice of fabrics and colors, whereas ready-made Austrian shades generally come in white or cream.

A special kind of traditional window is the bay window, found in many Colonial houses. These are real architectural assets, and can be treated in a number of ways to highlight their charm. Unless warmth and privacy are important, it's a good idea to use either sheer curtains of some sort, café curtains, or shades, rather than long, lined draw draperies. If there is a window seat, cover it with a cushion to harmonize with the curtains. If the seat is deep and wide enough to curl up on, add a few throw pillows for comfort. A bow window should be given a simple treatment. Long curtains in either plain or printed sheer fabric will always be attractive. If you prefer to keep the window uncovered most of the time, install a curved traverse rod. Or

53

use a plain rod, and attach rings to the top of the curtains so that they slide easily.

3. *Unusual windows*. Have you got a problem window? One that looks too small for the wall? One that is located halfway up the stairs, and looks out into an alley? Some basement windows that you need to decorate in making a recreation room? For every window, there is an attractive solution. A small window in a hall or stairway can be turned into a bright or amusing decorative feature. If it is recessed, put in two or three glass shelves to hold figurines, or seashells, or plants. Or attach a panel of stained glass—you can sometimes find these in junk shops. Or make your own stained glass by gluing bits of colored tissue paper onto the window, and covering the panes with a coat of varnish. You can buy paints for use on glass. However, unless you're sure of your artistic

Opposite: you can give a custom look to ready-made draperies by adding some trimming. Here, rows of ball fringe, applied to draperies, cornice, and roller shade, lend color to a window.

Left: pretty, small-paned windows are a decorating asset. Here, they've been trimmed with modified café curtains matching the tablecloth. If you have no separate dining room, it's a good idea to put the table near a window, creating a sense of "place" for dining, and profiting from the view.

install the rod higher than the frame, and cover the space with a valance or cornice. Better still, use a decorative brass or wooden rod with tie-back draperies.

Small windows near the ceiling of a basement room will look good with short, bright colored or patterned curtains. These can be of the draw type, or they can have inverted scallops at the top, and be hung like café curtains. In either case, run the rod slightly beyond the window frames so that the curtains will completely clear the windows when drawn, letting in as much light as possible.

You'll probably want curtains or draperies for most of your windows. Your next decision is between ready-made, custom-made, and those you make yourself. Obviously, the most expensive are custom-made ones, and you can quickly go into the red if you decide on these. Ready-made curtains and draperies are available in a wide range of colors, styles, and sizes. If you can't stand the thought of trying to make draperies, ready-mades are the obvious choice. If your windows are odd sizes, you may have to buy draperies slightly wider or longer than you need. A little extra width is no problem: you either use slightly wider rods, or you have slightly fuller draperies. Ideally, both panels of draw drapes combined should measure a foot more than the width of the window. This allows for a three to four inch overlap at the center, plus three to four inches return on either side. (The return is the part of the drapery from the corner of the rod to meet the wall.) If the draperies are too long, you can either shorten them, or install the rod slightly higher.

If you want to save money and still have

skill, it's wise to buy a separate piece of glass and paint your design on that. Frosted glass will effectively screen out an undesirable view.

To make a window appear wider than it is, put up a rod wider than the window, and hang opaque curtains or draw draperies. When opening them, pull them only as far as the window frame. This will suggest that the window extends farther than it actually does. Similarly, to make the window appear taller,

Right: it's often possible to buy both curtains and draperies that will match a bedspread. The bright colors of this quilted spread and matching draperies give this charming bedroom a lot of zest.

custom-made draperies, the obvious solution is to make them yourself. If you don't have a sewing machine, borrow or rent one. Admittedly, making draperies—especially lined ones—is a bit like sewing the Big Top. But once you get started, those apparent miles of seams go quickly. Your sense of accomplishment when you hang up the draperies will make all the effort seem well worth while.

When you set out to buy fabric—or ready-made curtains—you should take along a sample of your carpet or rugs, and wallpaper or paint, for comparison. Here are a few points to consider:

Dark fabrics tend to look darker when hung, because of the contrast of the bright light coming through the window. Soft and deep textures, such as velveteens and nubby weaves, will tend to look darker than a plain or satin-weave fabric of the same shade.

Your choice of curtain or drapery fabric will partly be determined by the style and mood of the room. For a formal room, which can be either modern or traditional, choose damask, faille, brocade, velveteen, or some other rich textured fabric. Many synthetics are suitable for formal rooms, and are generally less expensive than wool, silk, and the other natural fibers. For informal rooms, choose a plain or rough textured fabric, such as polished cotton, chintz, Indian Head, poplin, gingham, corduroy, or burlap.

Draperies, whether formal or informal, should be of medium- or heavy-weight fabric. Usually they are lined—mainly to make them hang better and guard against fading, but also to give a uniform appearance to the windows as seen from outside. Cotton sateen is the usual lining fabric. Many drapery fabrics, however, will hang well unlined; so if you're decorating a temporary home and may replace your draperies in a few years, you may not feel that a lining is worth the extra cost and bother.

56

Above: if you prefer the more modern look of large simple shapes, this restful-yet-cheerful design, repeated on the pillowcase, might be your choice of treatment for decorating a bedroom window.

For sheer curtains you can choose among marquisette, sheer nylon, ninon, fiberglass, organdy, dotted Swiss, and many other weaves. Ruffled tie-backs and crisscross curtains should be made of crisp fabrics, such as organdy; otherwise they will have a tendency to droop.

The vast majority of sheer fabrics can be washed. Some may shrink, however, so if you're in doubt about your chosen fabric, preshrink it before cutting. If you're buying ready-mades, allow for shrinkage, unless the curtains are guaranteed not to shrink. As for draperies, washing them is such a struggle that you'll probably want to have them dry cleaned, so you needn't make a point of buying washable fabric.

Don't overlook the possibilities of sheets as curtains. Today, sheets come in beautiful colors and patterns—too pretty to keep under cover. Use sheets to curtain your bedroom windows.

Other convertible ideas: terrycloth towels will make smart looking curtains for a small bathroom window; tea towels sewn together will make gay kitchen curtains. The main thing is to use your imagination. Don't feel confined to the suggestions you have read here, or anywhere else. Let your windows express your own creative self.

Furniture Sense

5

Comfort is what today's furniture is all about, and this cozy sofa—ideal for a family room—is an example. It consists of a cloth covered wood frame filled with thick foam cushions. A profusion of scatter pillows in gaily printed fabric add to the comfort. You can make the pillows yourself, with fabric remnants.

It would be great fun to go out and buy a houseful of furniture, armed with an enormous bank balance and, perhaps, gently guided by an interior decorator. Most of us, however, aren't in this happy position. We must buy furniture a bit at a time, starting with the bare essentials, and adding to them until we have all we need. Your acquisitions may be supplemented by cast-off items from relatives and friends. The end result is often a houseful of oddments: some attractive items, a few that you once liked but that now seem dreary, and a few real horrors that you keep vowing to replace—but with what? Perhaps you haven't reached this point as yet, and are still in the first stages of decorating—the cushions-on-the-floor-and-TV-tray phase. In either case, you must answer a number of questions about furniture needs and wants. Which items should I buy to last a lifetime? Where can I find furniture bargains? Is it possible to transform ugly pieces of furniture into attractive ones? Can I mix furniture styles successfully? How can I arrange my furniture in a way that is both attractive and functional?

When you're beginning to furnish a home, it's wiser to buy a few good pieces of furniture and add to them gradually than to buy a houseful of mediocre things you don't really like, and that will wear out quickly—or, perversely, *not* wear out and go on cluttering your home for years to come.

Your first essential, obviously, is a bed. This is one piece of furniture for which you should plan to pay a fair amount of money. You spend nearly one-third of your life in bed, and you should have one that gives your body the right kind of support. A good

59

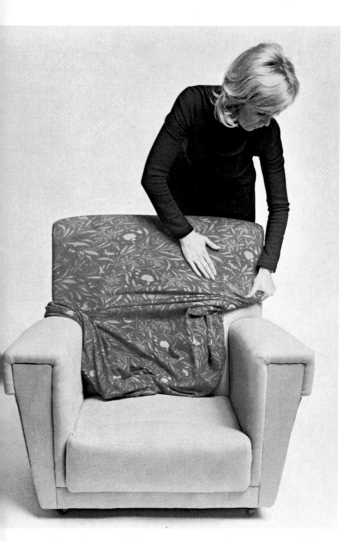

There's no quicker way to transform an ungainly or worn chair or sofa than by giving it a slipcover. A vivid print will camouflage its lines; a soft color will make a too-large piece look smaller. If you want to make a chair look less conspicuous, you can cover it with fabric matching the color of the walls or rug. You can also tie ill-matched furnishings together by covering them with the same fabric.

can contain either open coils or individually pocketed coils. If you are considering the open-coil type, you should bounce on it a bit to check that the springs do not rub together and squeak. Foam mattresses may contain either urethane foam or latex; the latter is considered generally less desirable than the former, but may be satisfactory if it is thick and dense. Solid mattresses, such as those found in bunk beds and sofa beds, do not give very good support.

You should buy both mattress and springs together if you possibly can. Putting a new mattress on old worn-out springs will tend to shorten the life of the mattress. Open-coil springs are much less expensive than box springs, but may perform equally well. However, they are rather unsightly, and collect dust. Flat springs tend to sag after a short time.

Convertible beds have an obvious advantage for people with little space, but, even if you have plenty of bedroom space for your family, you may want a sofa bed for a guest room. They're handy, but they generally don't provide good body support because the mattress and springs are thin to begin with, and the folding and unfolding of the bed takes its toll of them both.

If you're just starting to furnish a home, you may find that buying even the basics costs more than you can afford without going deeply into debt. Solution: settle for some entirely makeshift items. With a little ingenuity, and some paint or slipcovers, you can transform the most unpromising items into colorful and useful furnishings that will serve you well until you're ready to replace them with something better. You may even find that some of these stepchild furnishings will become permanent and valued.

Suppose, for example, that you buy a first quality mattress and box springs, a handsome and well-constructed sofa, and two beautiful lamps. The cost of these items, plus the cost of rugs, paint and wallpaper, a stove, and a refrigerator, has you in debt up to your ears. You still need a lot of other furniture, though —a dining room table, a chest of drawers,

night's rest will help you cope with everyday life. Conversely, a bed that does not support you properly will make you feel tired, and can even cause back trouble.

Generally speaking, a firm bed is better than a soft one. The only way to tell if a bed is right for you is to try it out. Lie on it, see if it supports all parts of your body equally well, and notice if it springs back into shape after you get up. Ask to see a cross section of the mattress. Most good mattresses are the inner-spring type, which

A room with an odd assortment of furniture was given unity and a new look by covering sofa, stool, and wing chair with the same black and tan check. The bright red-orange piping ties in with the lampshade trim and the scatter cushions, and emphasizes the lines of the wing chair. This room is a blend of modern and Early American styles.

chairs, bookshelves. You can't afford to buy what you want, but you must have something. With a little luck you may get some cast-offs from relatives and friends. Or you may find an item or two at the Salvation Army, or in junk shops. You may even find usable furniture sitting out on the street to be collected by the city. Few of these items are likely to be just what you had in mind, and most of them will be downright shabby. But don't despair. A coat of paint, a slipcover, even a bit of contact paper can work wonders

on unlikely objects. Here are some ideas.

An unsightly round occasional table may not be worth stripping and refinishing. Instead, cover it with a long circular cloth in felt, or some other substantial fabric, cut and sewn by you in a couple of hours. *Voila!* You've created something colorful on which to place your pretty lamp, an ashtray, and your wedding photo. The dismal dark brown bookshelves you find in a junk shop for $5 may be more than acceptable once you've stripped off the paint, and either stained it

Right: Victorian interiors can have a great deal of warmth and charm. Here, the ornate lines of the furniture are lightened by the fresh yellow and green of the color scheme, and the plain walls. A modern light fixture (background) harmonizes well.

Below: totally different in feeling is this ultramodern room in tones of creamy white, which manages to cater for an informal lifestyle in formal terms. The clean lines of the cushions are echoed in the perfectly simple clear plastic nesting tables.

or repainted it. An ancient sewing machine with curvy iron legs can be converted into an amusing table, minus the machine. Paint the iron part Chinese red or peacock blue, or whatever goes with your color scheme.

You can do wonders with paint and varnish. An antique finish is easy to do; your paint dealer can probably supply you with an antiquing kit and instructions. You

Above: formal modern furniture, inspired by the Roman Empire, complements reproductions of ancient pottery. The grouping of the *chaises longues* and table is underlined by an area rug.

Right and below: these pictures illustrate the different moods created by different textures. The modern room has an "active" mood achieved with dark vinyl flooring. leather sofa cushions, and lots of tubular steel. (Notice that most of the furniture is on casters, contributing to the feeling of activity). Below: warm tones of wood give a "settled" atmosphere. The heavy carved table legs contrast with the graceful lines of the bentwood chairs. Mixing furniture styles in this way can be most effective.

can also decorate wooden furniture with découpage, the application of cut-out designs, or with designs you stencil on it.

If you have a trunk—and who doesn't?— buy a piece of foam rubber, and cut it to fit the top of the trunk. Cover the whole thing with a piece of fabric. You have seating for one, or possibly two—not terribly comfortable seating, but it will do as a temporary measure. A trunk covered with a cloth can also serve as a place for your TV set, some books, or whatever you like.

One way to deal with an undesirable piece of furniture is to paint it or slipcover it the same color as the wall or the floor. It's astonishing how the most aggressively ugly chest of drawers or overstuffed chair will retreat "into the woodwork" with this treatment.

You can also use fabric to unify a room that's full of ill-matched furniture. Slipcover a sofa and one or two chairs with the same fabric, and you'll be surprised how odd shapes are made less conspicuous, and how the room no longer has a haphazard look.

This doesn't mean that furniture should necessarily be of the same style, however. Interesting rooms are furnished with pieces that complement each other, and not with those that repeat the same design with monotonous uniformity. The once popular living room furniture suite is, in general, to be avoided. Some of these may be well-designed, but they tend to make a room boring. They can, however, be livened up

by adding a few visual surprises to the room —for example, a red Victorian chair with a beige modern suite; or a starkly modern glass and aluminum cocktail table with a traditional brocade covered suite. Accessories can also help to liven up a room.

Many people end up with rooms containing a mixture of styles. They may wish they had the money to throw it all out, and do the whole room over in French Provincial, say, or Early American. Today, however, more and more people are realizing that the happiest decorating effects are often achieved through the mixing of styles, rather than through rigid adherence to one particular style. This is what makes modern decorating so exciting.

Of course, mixing styles has to be done with a certain amount of care if it is to be successful. You can't just buy whatever you like with no thought to how it will relate to

Left: an old bureau purchased for $10 was transformed by raising the carved top with a large piece of plywood, painting it with white enamel, and applying contact paper and new hardware.
Below: pastel gloss paint renews a table and mirror.

Right: don't be afraid to give *new* furnishings a decorative touch—for example, an ice cream soda painted on a refrigerator.

Above: a new look for an old table desk with blue and white paint.
Right: boldy patterned contact paper was used to cover this cabinet and mirror frame, adding color impact.

From Denmark: a clever furnishing plan for a one-room apartment, making maximum use of little space.

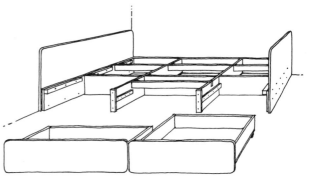

The main attraction of the room is the sitting-sleeping area: two mattresses and a shaggy rug, raised off the floor by a wooden stage concealing storage compartments. Drawers at the front of the unit hold bed linen. Other compartments, for less-often-used items, are accessible by lifting the mattresses. Simple lines and a fresh color scheme—apple green and white—help give an illusion of spaciousness. Notice how the straight lines of the furniture are softened by the clever use of accessories: ferns, a vase of flowers, some trinkets on the wall.

Above: the plan for the bed-living area showing the location of the storage compartments.

Below: the floor plan shows the relation of the bed-living area to the rest of the room.

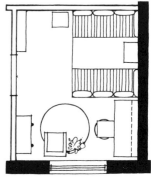

all of your other furnishings and furniture.

You must first establish a dominant mood for your room. The mood is partly determined by the color, of course, but it also depends greatly on the shape and size of your furniture. Do you want the room to be mainly formal in character? Romantic? Cozy? Cool and spacious in feeling? Informal? Exotic? Once you have an idea of the kind of room you want to create, you have a yardstick to apply to furniture you are considering buying. Some furniture styles create a certain mood strongly. For example, 18th-century English and French furniture is definitely formal, and even one or two pieces in these styles will tend to give a room a formal look. By contrast, Early American has an informal look. If you tried to mix Early American with Hepplewhite, for example, you would get a jarring effect, and

end up with no predominant mood because each would cancel the other out. (This mixture has probably been done successfully at one time or another by a skilled decorator, but it is not recommended for the amateur.)

Other styles of furniture seem to have more than one mood. Victorian has a cozy look, though too much of it in a room can be overwhelmingly cozy. The smaller Victorian pieces can have a romantic look, while the larger, heavier ones—such as desks and chests of drawers—are more formal. A richly carved Victorian desk in a severely modern living room will add a bit of warmth and an element of surprise, but will still be in keeping with the formal feeling of the room. A small Victorian chair will go well in a frilly bedroom. Chinese style furniture is more formal, and will look right in a simple modern room; but it can also lend itself to

The bed-living area is tailor-made for young ideas of comfort. It's an upholstered version of sitting on the floor. Dining is a matter of pulling over the three-decker end table. Appliquéd covers hold eiderdown quilts, or can be used as bedspreads.

a more informal scheme, with rattan chairs and floor cushions.

In mixing styles, be careful not to place pieces of different scale close together. For example, don't flank a massive modern sofa with delicate 18th-century end tables. There's no reason, however, why you shouldn't mix curvy lines with straight lines, or light wood with dark. Just don't overdo the mixture so that the room is a hodgepodge. The inexperienced decorator will usually find it advisable to stick to two furniture styles, making one of them contemporary.

Combining styles successfully demands a fairly experienced eye. There are no ready-made formulas to guide you. Some people have a natural flair for decorating, but the rest of us must learn to recognize good decorating possibilities. There's no need to learn by making expensive mistakes, however. You can learn a lot by just looking. Study the pictures and captions in this book. Study those in other decorating books and magazines. Visit model rooms in the stores. Visit museums and the beautiful historic homes open to the public. You'll gradually acquire a sense of design, and you'll get ideas that you can adapt to your own home.

Looking is part of your homework before you buy furniture. Planning is another part. As you acquire your furnishings, you must do some practical figuring to make sure the various pieces work well together. Taking a few measurements beforehand will help you avoid mistakes such as buying a dining table that extends to 10 feet when your dining alcove is only 9 by 9.

If you're moving into a new house or apartment, you can probably get a copy of the floor plan. Check the measurements given on the plan to make sure changes have not been made since they were printed. If no floor plan is available, draw your own. It's easy if you use graph paper. Establish a scale—$\frac{1}{2}$ inch to a foot, for example. Mark the location of all windows, radiators or other heating units, and electric outlets. Indicate which way the doors open.

Now, using another piece of graph paper,

Houses today tend to be smaller than those built in the past, and with the compact trend in housing has come the convertible trend in furniture. A striking example is this campaign-style desk, which converts into a dining table for eight people with the addition of four 15-inch leaves, placed between the front of the desk (far right) and the main section. The two top drawers of the desk are dummies; the bottom ones are real, and can be used to hold linens and silverware, or correspondence. The chair legs and backs fold up for easy storage, and the seats can be covered with the owners' choice of fabric.

draw and cut out small pieces corresponding to the furniture you now have. Make these to the same scale as your floor plan. Cut other pieces to correspond to furniture you intend to buy—either a specific item you are considering at the moment, or furnishings you would like to buy in the future. For example, you may intend sometime to buy a round cocktail table about three feet in diameter. Cut a scaled-down circle to repre-

sent it. For convenience in planning, color the pieces you haven't yet bought to make them show up clearly.

Arrange your paper furniture on your floor plan, and rearrange it to make a grouping that is both pleasing and functional. Take into consideration the traffic patterns in the room. Furniture should be placed so that people can move through the room easily. For example, in a dining room you should allow space for everyone to move his chair back far enough to get up and down from the table comfortably, and allow enough space around the table for bringing dishes to it and clearing them away.

In any room, furniture holding lamps, or any other breakable objects, should be

Right: a popular kind of furniture today is the furniture "wall"—a collection of shelf, drawer, and cabinet units chosen to suit the needs and taste of the owners. This handsome example has a cubbyhole desk, and a glassed-in cabinet for displaying some fine old books and china.

Below: a large room that doubles as living and dining room can benefit from a room divider like this one. The divider helps to create a conversation grouping, gives identity to the dining area, and more shelf space.

placed so that small children are not likely to bump into it. You needn't place all your living room furniture right against the wall, however—unless the room is tiny. It's much better to group some of the furniture together to make a conversation area, or a study area. Arrange a sofa and a couple of chairs so that people are close enough to talk comfortably, and provide a few tables at convenient spots for setting drinks down. If the room is large,

such a conversation grouping will be an inviting little "room within a room". If you have a fireplace, this can serve as the natural focal point of the grouping. Another grouping in the room might include a desk, a chair, and some bookcases; or a telephone table, mirror, and side chair; or—if the room is used for dining as well—a table and chairs.

If you have a high-fidelity system, you must, of course, take the placing of the

components into consideration. For serious listening, people should be able to sit facing the speakers, which should preferably be placed at ear level or slightly higher.

In planning a bedroom arrangement, make sure that you can open drawers and closet doors easily. If possible, place your dressing table in front of the window so that you'll get natural light on your face—important for applying daytime makeup.

While keeping practicality in mind, remember to balance the furniture in each room. Don't put everything at one end, leaving a lonely, empty space at the other. Neither should you strive for a symmetrical arrangement, with identical tables and lamps flanking the sofa, and so on. "Balance" really means to provide something of sufficient size or interest to complement another piece of furniture or group of furnishings that might otherwise attract all the attention. A large sofa on one wall, for example, could be balanced by a desk opposite. The balancing element needn't always be furniture. Brightly printed draperies, or a group of pictures, or some other accessories might do it. When arranging your floor plan, bear in mind that heights are an important factor in your decorating. Try to have a few tall objects in a room—bookshelves, a tall desk, a chest of drawers—to add variety.

Keep your floor plan and paper furniture for future reference when shopping for new items, or when considering a different arrangement of your existing furniture. As every woman knows, a change in furniture arrangement every now and then gives a room a lift. By trying the arrangement beforehand on the floor plan you can reduce backache to a minimum.

Any consideration of furniture arrangement leads eventually to the problem of storage facilities. Closets take care of many items, but there are always leftover items that don't seem to fit anywhere, and are likely to lie around in a clutter. This is particularly true after you have lived in a house for a while, and acquired more and more possessions. More toys, more hobbies, more kitchen utensils. Where does it all come from—and where can it all go?

First of all, take a good look at your existing storage space to see if you're using it efficiently. If you have a walk-in closet, you probably have some blank wall space inside that closet. Put up two metal strips and brackets for shelves. These can hold all kinds of things: shoe polishing equipment, a sewing basket, housecleaning supplies. While you're

Left: here, fabric and wallpaper were used for a storage area. Panels of bright green and white wallpaper on a wooden frame go along ceiling, and from ceiling to floor. Polka dot draperies hide all the shelves prettily.

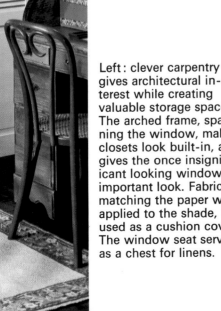

Left: clever carpentry gives architectural interest while creating valuable storage space. The arched frame, spanning the window, makes closets look built-in, and gives the once insignificant looking window an important look. Fabric matching the paper was applied to the shade, and used as a cushion cover. The window seat serves as a chest for linens.

looking in your closet, give a thought to the possibility of getting rid of some of the things you never use or wear.

Brackets-and-board shelves are useful in many parts of your home. You can design the arrangement to suit your own special needs. Some of the shelf systems available also have cabinets—handy for storing records, photographic equipment, or whatever else you need to store.

A few open shelves in the bathroom will provide storage space for towels—which come in such pretty colors that they make a decorative display. Bed and table linens, however, should be stored in a dry place, either a linen closet or a chest.

Storing kitchen utensils can be a problem. So many builders put cupboards so high you need a stepladder to reach the top shelf. One good idea is to use that top shelf for things you hardly ever need, such as Christmas tree ornaments. If your pots and pans overflow the remaining shelves, consider putting a sheet of pegboard on one wall, and hanging your most frequently used, or most decorative utensils on this board. If you have plenty of cupboards and drawer space, you may prefer to keep everything put away, and decorate your walls with pictures, a spice rack, or a shelf for your cookbooks. You can buy plastic turntables that sit inside cupboards to hold small items, such as condiments. A flick of the finger brings the items at the back around to the front, with no rummaging necessary.

Storing children's toys is a somewhat different problem. You can provide storage space and a system. Getting the children to use it is something else again. Shelves will hold books, games, and stuffed toys; but be sure they're low enough so the child can reach them easily. Large boxes are handy, particularly if the room will accommodate a number of them. Mark each one for different kinds of toys: dolls in one, coloring books in another, board games in another, and so on. Make the boxes as colorful as possible. Decorate them with magazine cutouts, and label each one "blocks", or "board games", or whatever it is intended to hold. If possible, use boxes that will slide under the bed, leaving plenty of play space for the children.

If you take a good look around your home, you will probably discover lots of wasted space that could be used for storage. The wedge shaped space under a stairway can accommodate anything from books to skiing equipment with the addition of a few shelves, a curtain, or—if one of the family is skilled at carpentry—a wooden partition. Many older houses have little niches that can be converted into shallow closets with the addition of folding doors.

If you're living in a small apartment or house with no spare nooks and crannies, and very limited closet space, take this fact into consideration when buying furniture. Instead of end tables and bedside tables, buy small cabinets to place beside the sofa and the bed. Wooden cubes can be used for storage and extra seating, and can be painted or covered with contact paper. Today, furniture manufacturers are producing many items geared to the needs of people in smaller houses. Take a good look around the stores before you buy. You may find many ready-made solutions to your storage problems—and you won't have to take a course in carpentry after all!

74

Left: boxes stacked in a diamond pattern give a lively look to a wall. Here, they're used in a children's room, but they could also be used in a study. Painting the boxes different colors—one color for each child—helps to keep their belongings separate.

Above: beauty and utility are combined in this attractive shelf unit. The glass jars keep ingredients handy and quickly identifiable. Contrasting paint emphasizes the pleasing arrangement of the shelves, and decoratively frames the plant, the teapots, and the inexpensive copy of Van Gogh's "Sunflowers." Left: a good way to store canned goods—rows of shelves one-can deep take up little space.

Effective Lighting

6

The right kind of lighting can make the dinner hour a festive occasion. This Tiffany style lamp casts a soft glow over the table—augmented by candles on the sideboard. Dark walls help to give the room a turn-of-the-century flavor, and also accentuate the lighting.

Lighting plays an important part in the beauty and comfort of your home. The most carefully planned color scheme, and the most attractive furnishings, will have little effect if a room is poorly lighted. Conversely, clever lighting can make a somewhat ordinary room look inviting. Inappropriate lighting can cut down efficiency, cause eyestrain, and even lead to accidents.

As you plan the lighting for your home you must, therefore, consider its practical value along with its decorative value. You must also consider the special qualities of each room—its function and its appearance, including the amount of daylight it receives. Nearly all rooms, and most hallways, already have some natural light from windows, and this should be taken into account when planning your artificial lighting. For example, a window at the top of a stairway will cause some glare, tending to throw the stairs into darkness if one is facing the window. In a case like this, additional, artificial light may be necessary, even in the daytime. The amount of daylight coming into a room will affect the quantity and the placement of your artificial lighting. Bear in mind, though, that you can exert some control over this available light—reducing it by means of various window treatments (see Chapter 4), or augmenting it by means of mirrors or by use of glossy paint.

The interaction of light and color is a subtle but powerful factor in planning your lighting. You've probably had the experience of buying some fabric, or a shade of lipstick in a store's florescent lighting, and then coming home to discover that seen in incandescent light, or in daylight, the color is much

Below: diffused lighting is provided in this kitchen by florescent tubes cleverly concealed behind the frosted glass ceiling panels. Direct lighting is well supplied by strip lighting placed under the cabinets.

Below: a strip of florescent light gives very good illumination for shaving and applying cosmetics. Below right: the two table lamps give good light for reading. Strip lighting plays up the draperies.

brighter and warmer. This is why you should always test a color under the lighting in your home. Two colors that contrast pleasingly by daylight, or by florescent light, can look almost identical, or clash appallingly, by incandescent light. The effect of color on light is somewhat more subtle. Cool colors, such as blue and green, will have a cooling effect on the light that strikes them; warm colors, such as red and yellow, will tend to make the light look warmer. Dark colors will absorb the light; lighter colors will reflect and diffuse it.

Shopping for light fixtures and lamps can be difficult because you rarely have a chance to evaluate the lamp in surroundings like those in your home. All the lamps are crowded together to make a setting that is unnaturally bright. You may easily be distracted by a lamp or fixture that is striking or unusual, and so overlook its practical limita-

Above: a decorative cornice is emphasized here by the use of concealed lighting, which accentuates its inverted scallops and pendants. The window treatment is ideal for apparently widening a room.

Right: if you have a collection to show off, consider the lighting carefully. Here, a pair of pottery jugs are displayed to advantage with the help of spotlights. The lamps can be moved along the track, which is fixed to the wall, and turned to various angles as needed or wanted.

tions. Below are a few general points to bear in mind when you shop for lighting.

Artificial lighting can be roughly divided into two categories: general diffusion, in which the light is released in all directions, and direct, in which the light is directed more specifically, so that you can see what you're doing when cooking, reading, sewing, or removing splinters from small fingers. Another use of direct lighting is to highlight certain featured objects, such as a painting, or a collection of shells, or an aquarium. Most rooms need both diffused and direct lighting. The proportion of each—and the placement of the fixtures—depends on the ways you use that room.

The kitchen must have plenty of light—for efficiency, and for safety as well. A good ceiling fixture is essential. It should be placed as close to the ceiling as possible for maximum diffusion of light into the whole room.

A recessed florescent tube will give good, and relatively cheap, diffused light; but be sure to buy "warm white" tubes, because the pure white tubes give off light that is unflattering—to food as well as to people. You will need direct lighting for work areas, where you'll be chopping onions, measuring ingredients, and washing dishes. Strip lighting can be fitted under cabinets to shine directly onto the work surface. Alternatively, attach small spotlights to the wall—the kind that will swivel as needed. If you normally eat your evening meal in the kitchen, you may also want a hanging lamp over the table to be used instead of, or in addition to, the overhead diffused lighting. If you only eat breakfast and lunch in the kitchen, you probably won't need any additional lighting.

Dining room lighting can be a controversial matter. You may like the romantic glow of candlelight, but if you restrict the dining room lighting to a few candles on the table, you may get remarks from your husband about accidentally buttering his tie. By all means use candles on the table—they give a lovely warm glow—but supplement them with additional light. A small lamp on the sideboard, or a couple of wall sconces, will give that bit of extra light you need in coping with an artichoke or a bony fish, without spoiling the romantic effect of the candles. Be wise, also, in your choice of candle holders. Beautiful as they are, tall candelabras can be rather bothersome if you have to peer through them to see each other. Put Aunt Cornelia's heirlooms on the sideboard, or on the living room mantel. Today, you have a choice of many beautiful low candleholders that will help you light your table effectively. Incidentally, if you plan to eat by candlelight often, consider painting or papering your dining walls a dark color—for example, dark green. It will accentuate the glow of the candles, and give a formal atmosphere.

For most family meals, however, you'll want an electric fixture, hanging fairly low over the table, and directing light down onto it. High, diffused lighting tends to give a rather cool atmosphere to a dining room. The traditional Scottish way of lighting meals was to have a hanging rise-and-fall lamp over the table. There are many modern versions of this, suitable for various kinds of decor. An additional advantage of this kind of lighting is that you can use the dining table for the children's homework, for games, for sewing, or for any other activity requiring ample direct light.

Living room lighting is more complex, and can vary greatly according to the family's lifestyle, and, of course, the mood and style of the decor. Some people like the general, diffused light provided by an overhead fixture; others prefer the more intimate lighting achieved with a number of table or floor lamps placed throughout the room. Even if you have an overhead lamp, you'll need several other lamps in the room for people to use while reading, knitting, or doing a jigsaw puzzle. Such lamps should be placed so

Above: two small lamps reflect light off a wall, just above the TV set. Some additional light in a room reduces glare when the television is on. Below: another use of a spotlight for display purposes. Notice, also, how books help to enliven a room with their colored bindings.

Above : pools of light give an intimate look to this living room—the ideal atmosphere for conversation. A dimmer switch will enable you to adjust the level of lighting in the room to suit the particular occasion.

Left : strong, direct light is needed for a work area—whether for writing, sewing, or model airplane building. An additional light source (upper right) cuts glare.

that the light falls over the shoulder, and illuminates the whole working area.

Many living rooms today are used principally for watching television. When watching television in the evening, you should have at least one lamp turned on, preferably one located to the side of, or behind, the TV so that the reflection won't interfere with the picture.

Dimmer switches are a great help in adjusting the lighting in a room from bright enough to read the newspaper, down to a soft glow for after-dinner conversation. They're not expensive, and they can actually help you save on your electricity bill by cutting down on unnecessary light. Alternatively, buy lamps that have three way switches, so that you can control the light to some degree.

In the bedroom you'll need a lamp on either side of the bed. If you like to read in bed, these should be flexible and of the spotlight type, so that they won't keep your partner awake when you want to read. If you use the bathroom mirror in applying makeup, you needn't put more than one small lamp on your dressing table; but if you use the dressing table mirror, you should flank it with two good lamps that shine on your face, not on the mirror. Plain cylindrical lamps of frosted glass, in a warm tone, are a good choice. Make sure, too, that your full-length mirror has sufficient light so that you can see your reflection clearly.

Small children need a good overhead fixture to light the whole room so they can see all around to find their runaway cars. A bedside lamp is a good idea, too. Tiny tots need one when they're having bedtime stories read, so they can sit up and see the pictures. It should be a lamp that they can switch on from the bed so that they don't get frightened when they wake up at night.

The bathroom generally needs some kind of overhead fixture giving enough light that you can see to clean around the basin and toilet—plus bright light around the mirror for shaving and applying cosmetics. Two florescent tubes on either side of the mirror

Above: simple, functional spotlights give light for reading or needlework. Another light shines through the painted glass window set into the wall above open shelves holding a number of plants.

Right: graceful, carpeted steps leading into an enclosed porch have concealed lighting, which not only acts as a safety precaution, but also highlights the shape of the steps, and the pleasing texture of the stone wall.

Above: light fantastic—
a plywood butterfly
brightens a bare wall.
Light bulbs are attached
under the wings.

Left: two Art Nouveau
lamps form part of a
decorative composition
on a side table. Muted
green and white make
a restful color scheme.

Below: a theatrical look
for a bathroom—dressing
room lights around the
mirror are practical, and
their dramatic effect is
well-suited to the bold
and splashy red and
yellow color scheme.

will do the job well; or you might prefer to use theater dressing room bulbs around the mirror. Bathroom lights should, ideally, have a pull-chain switch—safer for wet hands.

Speaking of switches, it's a very good idea to have two-way switches in areas such as stairs, long corridors, garages—in fact, anywhere it's useful to be able to turn the light on or off from more than one place.

Don't forget your outdoor lighting. Nearly all houses are equipped with front and back porch lights, but you may also need other lights outside if you have some steps leading up toward the house that won't be illuminated by the porch light. Besides providing safety, outdoor lights can serve a decorative function. If you have a pretty garden, why not install a few lights to highlight it?

Finally, here are a few things to bear in mind when purchasing a lamp. Give particular attention to the shade, because its color, shape, and material will affect the amount and direction of light that it gives. For example, a tubular shade will cast a

Left: golden browns in this traditional dining room are complemented by the red shade on the hanging lamp. Lighting fixtures that cast a pale diffused light toward the ceiling should be avoided in dining rooms.

Above and right: this flexible hanging lamp is fixed to a ceiling track so it can slide from the side of the room to the center, as well as moving up and down. Above it is shown adjusted to provide light for embroidery work. An old-fashioned bell pull hides the cord. At right, it lights a dinner table.

downward light over a small area. The more flare in the shade, the larger the illuminated area. A light colored cloth shade will give more light than a dark paper or metal shade. Both lamp shades and ceiling fixtures should conceal the bulb from the normal lines of vision. If the bulb is not well concealed, you should buy a soft-light one to cut glare.

If you can't find the kind of shade you want, why not try making one yourself? There are many different booklets giving directions, and you can find frames of all shapes and sizes, binding tape, enamel paint, pins, trimming, glue—in fact, all the equipment you will need—in most department stores. Making your own lamps from wine bottles, vases, or figurines, is even more satisfying. You needn't make your own lamps and shades to be creative with lighting, however. Like a stage designer, you have the opportunity to create whatever atmosphere you want in a room simply by choosing and arranging the lights you use with care and imagination.

Designed for Living

7

There's no reason to restrict the dining room to dining—it can be a place for family games, for homework, for sewing, or for any other activity for which you need a flat surface. This dining room is a pleasant place partly because of its accessories, including a collection of china.

Once you've finished your basic decorating, you want to relax and enjoy living in it. At first, it's a bit like owning a new car: you're afraid of scratching the paint. You make resolutions never to leave anything lying around, always to file correspondence the moment you've read it, and to make the children put their toys away when they finish playing. In practice, life simply isn't like that. A home that is too tidy and cleared away has a sterile, unlived-in look. So you will probably be much happier as you are.

Remember, comfort is one of the main factors in making a home attractive. Take another look at the lighting, and add a couple of lamps where people seem to be trying to read in semidarkness. If a chair seat is too deep for people to sit in comfortably, add a cushion or two. If your dining room furniture is arranged so that people keep bumping into the sideboard, change it.

Discomfort needn't be so obvious. It can also be subtle and psychological. A blue lampshade may be sending out cold vibes, making you feel vaguely uncomfortable without knowing why. See if changing it for a white or yellow one makes a difference.

As you continue to live in your home, you will make many additions and changes. Your decor will reflect your developing tastes and changing lifestyle. When your children reach their teens, for example, you may decide to convert part of the basement into a recreation room. When they finish their schooling, you'll have a bit more money for indulging your taste in china figurines, or antiques.

One part of decorating that is especially fun is adding accessories. When you first

An array of plants gives a house a fresh look— whether it's as simple as the window box this mother and daughter are planting (above), or as elaborate as the tropic-style terrace at right.

start your decorating, you'll probably already have a few cherished items that will alleviate the bare look. As the years go by, you'll have the pleasure of gradually acquiring more pretty and colorful accessories that will give your home the unique stamp of your own personalities. Be imaginative in the choice and display of accessories. If you already have too many ashtrays, fill one with some polished pebbles, and set it on a table under a lamp. Make a small hooked rug and hang it on the wall for a bright touch of color and interesting texture. Fill an empty perfume bottle with colored water, and place it on a window sill where it will catch the light. If you have a beautifully carved chess set, leave it out on display. Group a few brass candlesticks in front of a mirror; you get double the effect and double the candlelight. Accessorize your kitchen with tall jars filled with pasta, dried beans, and nuts.

Pictures, of course, are important accessories. You can get inexpensive—but often

Below: you can transform a plain stairway with a few plants placed at various levels (an arrangement not recommended for families having small children or large pets). A trailing plant will add a touch of color and pattern to the hallway.

well done — reproductions in many art museums. Some of these are already framed. If not, you can often find suitable ready-made frames. Or, frame them with glass and colored adhesive tape. If someone in the family is a good photographer, have some black and white prints made (much cheaper than color prints), and arrange them on a bulletin board. Change the pictures every now and then.

Few accessories do more for a room than flowers and plants—real ones, not plastic. If you have a flower garden, you can have cut flowers from early spring to late fall, depending on the part of the country in which you live. Put them throughout the house—not just in the living and dining rooms. You needn't always make big, elaborate displays. A few daisies in a pretty bottle on the bathroom windowsill, a mug of marigolds in the kitchen, a single rose floating in a shallow bowl on a bedside table—each can add a lovely touch of life and color.

During the winter months, cut flowers

89

must be obtained from the florist at considerable expense. Substitute dried flowers. They're no trouble at all, and they last for years. A good florist can supply you with a variety of pretty dried leaves and blossoms, which you can arrange and rearrange time after time. At your library or bookstore, you can probably get a book telling you how to grow and dry your own flowers. It's cheap, fun, and good value. If you sow the seeds in the garden first, you'll have a summer's pleasure from them while they're growing.

If you have a green thumb, you probably already grow some indoor plants. If not, consider getting some. Plants make an enormous difference in a room. Even a few pots of herbs on the kitchen windowsill will provide a welcome bit of greenery. A variety of shiny leaved specimens massed together on a low table will have a dramatic effect.

House plants need care and attention. If your plants turn sickly, you are probably mistreating them in some way. Start with easy-to-grow varieties, such as grape ivy and philodendron. Consult the nurseryman about the care and feeding of any plants you buy. Keep a sharp eye on the amount of sun they get. In winter, plants may become starved for sunlight; in summer they should, in most cases, be moved back into the room away from the windows, so that they don't get the direct rays of the sun. Wipe the leaves

The generation gap is a good idea—at least when it comes to planning your home. Above, grownups enjoy a quiet dinner on their own. If children have attractive, comfortable rooms, they'll be glad to spend time there. The L-shape of the room at right is well-suited to the two girls, each of whom has a distinct area for her own possessions, decorations, and clutter. It's like having two separate rooms, but chummier.

gently every week or so with a mixture of milk and water; plants don't like to be dusty. More house plants are killed by overwatering than by underwatering, especially in winter. Keep the soil just moist, and do not leave the pot standing in a bowl or saucer of water.

If you live in an apartment, and want a garden, you can plan a window box that will flower from early spring until frost. Plant crocus, daffodils, and tulips in the fall, and the first of these will appear in March or April. Then one will follow the other until it's time to plant for summer. Geraniums are a good choice for summer; they're colorful and easy to grow.

One last word about plants: don't dismiss the notion that talking to them helps. People

who talk to their plants seem to get excellent results. Anyway, it can't hurt.

"Talking" brings us to a very important aspect of your home environment, namely, the sounds in it. Today, most of us have to live our lives against a constant background of noise—the roar and screech of traffic; the drone of the vacuum cleaner; the clatter of school locker doors. A certain amount of noise is inevitable, but you can make your home considerably more attractive by controlling noise as much as possible. You may be surprised to find that a quiet atmosphere will improve everyone's disposition.

If you make the children's room an attractive place to play, you should be able to persuade them to confine their noisier games to that room, leaving the living room free for adult conversation. Try to arrange a quiet hour or so when your husband (and perhaps you yourself) gets home from work. A chance to read the paper, and have a drink in peace and quiet, will have a wonderfully soothing effect. Try to run the vacuum and the dishwasher at times when they won't interfere with talk, music, or study.

TV is one of the worst culprits in the noise making department. For those watching the program, it's entertainment; for those trying to talk or have a pleasant meal, it's noise. If at all possible, put the TV in the recreation room or guest room, or some other room with a door, so that the noise won't pervade the living-dining-kitchen area.

Left: if you have a would-be Tarzan in the family, give him scope to indulge his adventure fantasies. A rope ladder attached to the ceiling, and some boxes to climb, help to make this room an exciting hideaway for a growing boy.

Right: gay colors and lots of shelf space for storing and displaying toys are two attractive features of this children's room. The large blackboard is an outlet for artistic expression.

If yours is a musical family, a room fitted with acoustical tiles on the ceiling—and possibly the walls as well—is almost a necessity. That way, your fledgling violinist can get through those first few abrasive years without sending you into a rest home. For hi-fi enthusiasts, acoustic tiles are obviously out, because they deaden sound. A system of scheduled listening hours, and/or a set of headphones, may help the family keep music a pleasure instead of a nuisance.

A quiet place for study is important from the time your first child brings home his multiplication tables to the time your last one takes final high school exams. That's a lot of years of homework. You can set up a study area in a bedroom or in the dining room, but make sure it's possible to keep that area quiet when your young students are working. It should be some distance from

the TV and hi-fi sets. When the student is working, both loud arguments and great hilarity should be kept to a minimum. Most children, and adults too, will learn to concentrate with normal domestic background noise, but not with loud, aggressive noises.

If you are fortunate enough to have a room that can be used mainly for study, you can do a number of things to make it quieter. Acoustic tiles on the ceiling will help. A thin layer of cork on one wall will also help. Other sound absorbers are a soft rug, and heavy curtains.

If you create an environment that is comfortable for the family, the chances are that it will be comfortable for your guests. Some houses that are beautifully kept have an atmosphere that does not help either the family or visitors feel at ease. The first requirement for entertaining is comfort—not

Below: tiny children also enjoy drawing on a blackboard, if it's put at their level. This one is set into a kitchen counter, so that Baby can entertain himself under Mother's supervision while she fixes dinner.

just bodily comfort, but psychological comfort as well. There should be furniture for all shapes and sizes of people. There should be tables within easy reach for drinks and ashtrays. There should be a few books, papers, and magazines easily at hand so that they look as though they are meant to be picked up. The room should not be drafty, but neither should it be too hot. In this controversial matter, however, there are no real guidelines. One man's sauna bath is another's deep-freeze. So the best thing to do is simply to ask the guest if he finds the temperature comfortable, and adjust it if necessary.

When you have overnight guests, you have a few more things to remember. His own drinking glass in the bathroom will give the guest a more pleasant option than sticking his head under the tap, or swallowing tooth-paste. A washcloth is a thoughtful touch, in case the guest hasn't brought his own; and, of course, you'll provide bath and hand towels. Some light reading beside the bed will often be appreciated, as well as an extra pillow, in case he prefers to sleep with two.

Children will find that their friends enjoy coming for a visit if there are plenty of games, books, and toys in the room. Comfortable cushions on the floor, and bright colors, help to give an air of relaxed friendliness that will make them feel at home.

Safety is of the utmost importance in any home, and particularly if there are children or elderly people. When laying rugs on smooth floors, make sure that they won't curl up or slip, and send people flying. Rugs at the top of the stairs should be fastened down securely. Do not overpolish wood and vinyl floors, or they will be a hazard.

This handy storage man is only one of the ingenious decorating ideas you'll find in the following 32 pages. They include some clever solutions to decorating problems, some useful furnishings and accessories you can make yourself, and some suggestions you can adapt to your own requirements.

Lamp cords, and cords from other electrical equipment, should not be run under the rug. Unless the appliance is right next to the socket, and the cord lying in a place where no one could possibly trip on it, you should staple the cord along the lower edge of the baseboard. If you have small children or pets, cover unused sockets with tape.

One continually hears warnings to keep medicines and poisons out of reach of small children, but every year many children still become ill, and some die, because of inadequate precautions in storing these things. Keep your medicines, cleaning fluids, and insecticides far out of a child's reach. A simple lock on cabinets holding these items will give you peace of mind.

Make sure that you have adequate fire fighting equipment. A chemical fire extinguisher on each floor is a good idea. Make sure everyone in the house knows where it is, and how and when to use it. When frying foods, keep a large lid handy to clap on the pan if the fat starts burning. Never add water to burning fat.

Fortunately, serious accidents seldom happen. But spills, stains, and dirt are a constant fact of domestic life. No matter how many labor-saving appliances you have, you'll still have to spend a great deal of time cleaning house. To save yourself from cleaning more than is absolutely necessary, practice some preventive housekeeping. Spray curtains and upholstery with a fabric protector, which provides a shield against dirt, and makes cleaning easier. Wash painted surfaces often; paint that is washed at frequent intervals will not need repainting so soon. Carpets that are given an occasional shampoo will wear longer, and when you have to clean up a spill, the newly cleaned spot won't show up so alarmingly against the rest of the carpet. Rugs and carpets should be vacuumed thoroughly at least once a week, with intermittent touch ups as required, depending on the amount of cat hairs, cigarette ash, and squashed crayons you must contend with. Rubber mats just inside the front door and kitchen door will keep mud from being tracked throughout the house.

In the bathroom, keep scouring powder by the tub (unless you have very small children) for each member of the family to use after a bath. You can make cleaning the bathtub ring almost fun with a nylon net puff. Run a gathering thread down the center of a strip of net, and gather it up into a ball. This works effectively even without scouring powder. Wiping up spills quickly when they occur, and dusting where needed every day, will make the occasional overall cleaning less daunting.

In our mobile society, the chances are that your first home will not be your last. In fact, it may be the first of several homes you'll decorate and enjoy. Your needs—and your taste—will change over the years. Even if you stay in the same house throughout your adult life, you'll make changes and improvements. You can eventually correct your mistakes, if any, and you can apply new knowledge of fabrics, colors, and styles, as you gain confidence in your own judgment. Every time you create a new flower arrangement for the hallway, or buy some new guest towels, or crochet another dressing table cloth, you'll again experience the pleasure of home decorating.

Project
Section

Decorative Doors

Doors can play a big part in your decorating scheme, if you use a little imagination. If your doors are uninteresting slabs, why not adapt some of the ideas shown here? An enormous range of wallpapers, paints, and molding strips can help you do the job.

The octagonal star design on the opposite page is well-suited to a formal decor. Copy the design on a large piece of graph paper,

Below: a Pop Art effect such as these gigantic red waves can be achieved with high gloss paint and stencils, which were used to make the white areas.

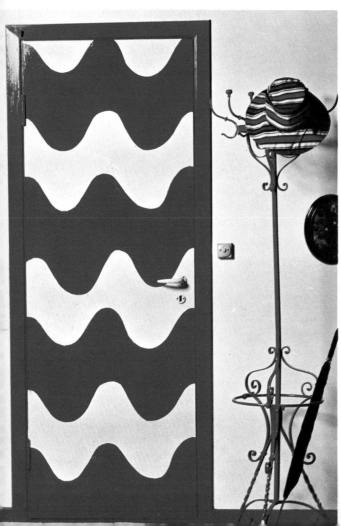

Right: you can give architectural interest to a plain door with strips of molding applied in interesting patterns.

Left: applying glue to a door in a thin line, to which molding is stuck.

Below: a boldly modern interpretation of Victorian design. The wallpaper sweeps over the door, which has been outlined by painting the frame glossy dark green.

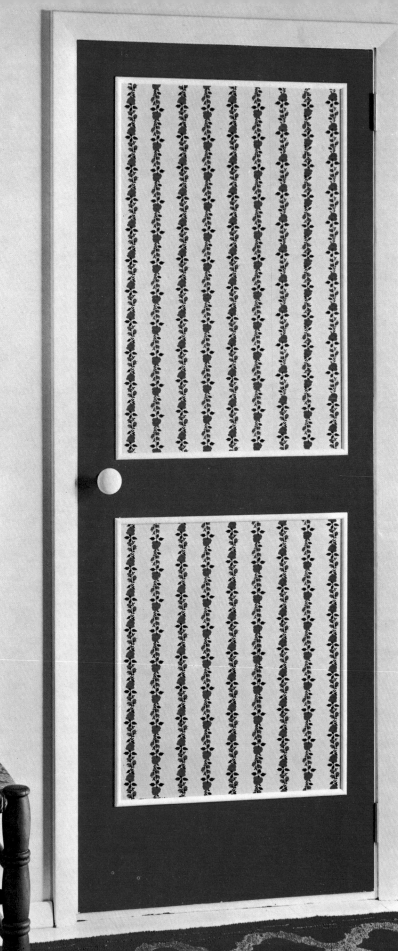

Left: this provincial style door uses printed wallpaper, red paint, and cream colored molding.

Below: the same basic idea in a formal design with fancy molding.

Below right: fresh blue, green, and white in a more modern variation.

enlarging it to the correct size. Measure the total length of the strips, and multiply by three to determine the amount of molding you'll need. Trace the outside edge of each strip's location onto the unpainted door (taken off its hinges). Measure and cut all the strips (you will need a miter box for this), and glue them in place. When the glue has dried, paint the door and rehang it.

A combination of paint, molding, and wallpaper (or adhesive plastic) can make a strikingly effective door. To create a fancy design, such as the one in the center, play around with bits of molding until you get a design you like. Tape the molding in place on a sheet of paper, and draw around the outside edges. Remove the molding, and cut out the pattern, cutting slightly inside the line. Trace the pattern onto wallpaper or adhesive plastic. Apply the paper to the painted door, and then glue onto it the pieces of molding.

Curtain Corner

The disappearance of the dining room in modern houses, and the consequent necessity of eating in the living room or the kitchen has tended to make dining less of an "occasion." If you live in a house or apartment without a dining room, and would like to restore some elegance to the dinner hour, consider curtaining off part of the living room as shown in these photographs. The

The instant dining room: A sheer, gaily printed curtain on a curving track can be opened in any direction, or closed to create a feeling of intimacy. The red and orange print harmonizes with the cushions and the table settings, and contrasts with the cream colored furnishings.

soft folds of the curtains give a feeling of warmth and intimacy, while the sheerness of the fabric keeps you from feeling claustrophobic.

Unless you're handy at carpentry, you'll probably want to hire someone to attach the circular track to the ceiling. You can, however, make the unlined curtains yourself.

You can adapt this idea in various ways to suit your own situation. A large kitchen can be partitioned with a straight curtain wall to make a dining area. By turning off the kitchen light, and turning on the lamp in the dining area, you get instant seclusion from the pots and pans. A curtain wall can also provide some privacy in a room shared by two children; or it can be used to create a sewing corner in your bedroom.

101

Ways with Plants

A carpenter's box painted a sunny yellow, and suspended from the ceiling by two chains, makes a sturdy, handsome holder for several plants, left in their individual pots. Choose one plant that will fall gracefully over the side of the box, such as the ivy. If you can't find a carpenter's box, make your own, using two paddle-shaped cutting boards, three plain boards, and a broom handle.

More ways to hang plants: put the pot in a braided straw holder, and suspend it from a wall bracket. If you do macramé, you can make endless variations of this type of sling. A shiny old fireman's helmet makes a striking holder for a trailing plant, such as ivy or philodendron. An old birdcage, with some of the bars removed, would also make an interesting holder for trailing plants.

A pretty plant deserves an attractive holder. Show off your plants with holders of various shapes, styles, and materials. Here are a few examples. Use your imagination for others.

The gleaming copper and brass bucket is well-suited to large plants with dark shiny leaves, such as poinsettias. It would also do admirably for an orange tree.

Left: antique brass and copper, straw matting, and shiny leaved plants provide an interesting contrast of textures.

Right: a braided straw sling, a white pot, and a tropical plant stand out against a red wall.

Above : a fanciful use of
an old fireman's helmet
as a holder for some ivy.

Left : painted a butter-
cup yellow, a carpenter's
tool box makes a charming
holder for several plants.

The Adap-table

The simple lines of the Parsons table (named for the Parsons School of Design) make it adaptable to any kind of decor. You can simply paint it with a high gloss paint to match your color scheme—but why not do something more imaginative? With some interesting trimming, a stencil, wallpaper, fabric, or patterned contact paper, you can make your table a real conversation piece.

Above: Chinese red initials on a putty colored background harmonize with sofa and Oriental rug.

Above: shiny metal washers give an interesting kind of texture to this small table. The washers can be easily applied with either iron glue or Duco cement.

Left: brilliant blue and emerald green go together very well, as do the modern and Victorian furnishings.

The table shown far left was decorated with the owners' initials, taken from a stencil sheet. The one in the center was trimmed with fancy braid, attached with white casein glue, and mitered at the corners. The braid, repeated on draperies, valance, and shade, gives the table an old-fashioned look, in keeping with the Victorian chairs and framed fashion plates. A strikingly modern note in traditional surroundings is provided by the table above, which was first painted brown, then covered with one-inch metal washers. (The proportions of the table will dictate the size of the washers, which must fit evenly.)

Wallpaper makes an attractive covering for a Parsons table. Protect the surface with three coats of polyurethane gloss.

105

For play or display, this easily constructed box is a winner. Set on casters (above), the boxes are fun for children to play in. Stacked together (left), they provide shelf space for your books and records.

Right: variations of the box, painted a crisp blue and white, and joined with metal brackets, make a handy sewing corner.

The "Everything" Box

These handy, versatile boxes can be easily made by even a novice carpenter. For an 18-inch cube, open at one end, cut 5 squares of $\frac{1}{2}$-inch plywood: 4 measuring 18 inches square, and one measuring $18\frac{1}{2}$ inches square (the bottom). Glue, then nail the sides together. Place the *side* of one board on the *edge* of the next, all around, so that when all four sides are joined, the box measures $18\frac{1}{2}$ inches on each side. Use finishing nails to join them, and be sure to drive the nails

exactly straight to avoid splitting the plywood edge you're nailing into. Glue and nail the $18\frac{1}{2}$-inch square to one end of the box.

For a lid, cut another $18\frac{1}{2}$-inch square. Glue four strips of $\frac{1}{2}$-inch beading to the square, so that the outside edge of the beading lies $\frac{1}{2}$ inch in from the edge of the square. The beading will fit just within the sides of the box, and keep the lid from slipping. You can drill a finger hole in the center of the lid.

Alternatively, you can make a hinged door

for the box, using a piece of plywood measuring $17\frac{1}{2}$ by $17\frac{1}{2}$. This is fixed just inside the opening, using concealed hinges on the right side, and a cupboard catch on the left. Drill a finger hole, or attach a knob.

The work area shown above uses open and closed storage cubes made of $\frac{3}{4}$-inch chipboard, and joined to each other with metal brackets. The units on the right are oblong boxes, constructed in the same way as the cubes, but deep.

Collector's Table

Here is a practical, easy-to-make, glass-topped table that can be used to display a collection of treasured objects—perhaps some exotic butterflies, a mineral or fossil collection, a selection of foreign stamps.

To make the table, you will need:
a length of planed softwood—4 inches wide, $\frac{1}{2}$-inch deep, and 7 feet 6 inches long.
another length of planed softwood—2 inches square and 6 feet long.
a piece of plywood $\frac{1}{2}$-inch thick, measuring 1 foot 6 inches by 2 feet $2\frac{1}{2}$ inches. (Buy $\frac{3}{4}$-inch plywood if you are displaying rocks or other heavy objects.)
a length of beading $\frac{1}{2}$-inch thick, 6 feet long.
a piece of glass $\frac{1}{4}$-inch thick, measuring 1 foot 6 inches by 2 feet $2\frac{1}{2}$ inches. Have the edges smoothed by the glazier.
16 no. 8 *wood screws*, $1\frac{1}{2}$ inches long, and $\frac{1}{2}$ pound of $\frac{3}{4}$-inch *finishing nails*.

You will also need: a good *saw*, a *hammer*, a *screwdriver*, an *awl*, a *hand drill*, *glue*, *plastic wood*, *sandpaper*, *brushes*, and *paint*.

Cut the 6-foot length of 2-inch square timber into 4 pieces (the legs), each 18 inches long. Make sure that the cut edges are perfectly square. Cut the 7-foot 6-inch length into 4 lengths (the sides): 2 measuring 2 feet 3 inches long, and 2 measuring 1 foot 6 inches long. Take one of the short sides (A in the diagram), and cut $\frac{1}{4}$ inch from one long edge, thus reducing its depth and providing a recess on which the glass top will fit, enabling it to be lifted off easily.

Fit two of the legs to Side A, placing them flush with the top and outer edges. Mark the positions of the 2 screws at each end of the side—1 inch up from the bottom, 1 inch in from the sides, and $\frac{3}{4}$ inch down from the

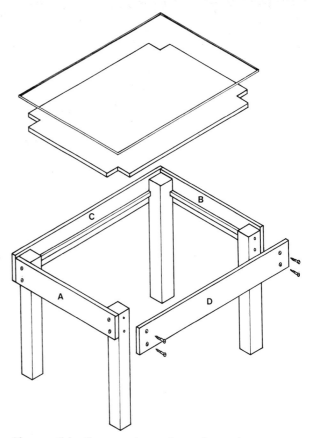

Above: this diagram shows how the various parts of the glass-top table are assembled.

Right: a beautiful display of colorful butterflies makes this simple table a real conversation piece. The butterflies were mounted on squares cut from a polystyrene ceiling tile, glued to the plywood base.

top. Drill 4 holes in the side, using a no. 8 wood bit in the hand drill. Using a counter-sink bit, widen the holes on the facing side so that the screw heads will fit flush with the side. Before inserting the screws, use the awl to pierce the legs where the screws will enter.

Attach the other 2 legs to Side B in the same way, but place the legs $\frac{1}{4}$ inch down from the top to allow for the glass. The upper screws on B are placed 1 inch from the top.

Cut the beading into 2 lengths of 1 foot 2 inches for the ends, and 2 lengths of 1 foot 10 inches for the sides. These strips will be a support for the plywood base on which the collection is displayed, and should be placed at a depth appropriate for the objects. For a butterfly collection, a depth of $2\frac{1}{2}$ inches is desirable. A mineral collection would require an extra $\frac{1}{2}$ to 1 inch, while a stamp collection would only need a total depth of 1 inch. Glue the beading to sides A and B, exactly the same distance down from the tops of the legs. Glue the beading to sides C and D at the same depth, allowing $2\frac{1}{2}$ inches at each end for the table legs and the edges of the adjacent sides. Now nail the beading to the sides at 2-inch intervals, using the finishing nails.

Attach sides C and D to sides A and B, inserting the screws in the same way as described for A, but placing them $1\frac{1}{2}$ inches from the ends. (Sides C and D overlap the edges of sides A and B, as shown in the diagram.) The upper edges of sides C and D are $\frac{1}{4}$ inch above the tops of the legs (as with Side B).

Cut 2-inch squares from the corners of the plywood base. Lower the base into position on the beading supports. If the base proves to be slightly oversize, you can sand it down to fit. Nail the base to the beading.

Use plastic wood to fill in the screw ends, nail holes, and any gaps in the joints. When the plastic wood is dry, sand the table smooth, and paint it. Arrange the display objects and cover them with the glass top.

Picture a Wall

Do your family photos and snapshots languish in a drawer, or in an album you seldom open? Why not put them on display? You can do this inexpensively and effectively.

A junk shop, a bazaar, or your own attic might yield some old-fashioned wooden frames to make an attractive grouping such as the one shown at right.

Below, a picture wall is easy to create with the help of boxes and their lids, and several colors of paint. You can mount the pictures on top of the boxes, or cut out the boxes and use them as mats, with the pictures attached to the underside.

Brighten a bare white wall with an assortment of black and white color prints mounted edge to edge on a matching white board. You can use double-sided tape or tiny map pins to attach the photographs.

Above: a charming
group of family photos in
old frames gives a warm,
homey touch to a simple
modern study corner.

Left: boxes give a sur-
face interest to this wall,
and make inexpensive
frames for the photos.

Right: photos make a
big splash when they are
massed together, as here.

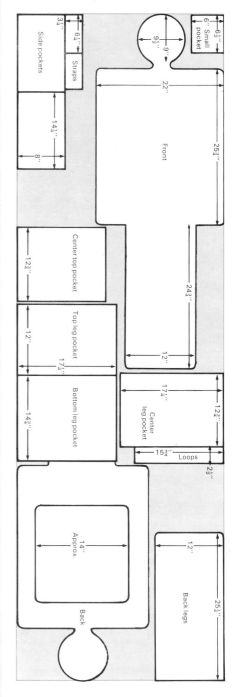

Here's a handyman who'll help you solve some of your storage problems. You can construct the storage man yourself, using sturdy denim. Pockets pleated at the sides easily accommodate a variety of things. Below: this cutting plan shows one way to cut out the various pieces that make up the storage man. A pattern is needed to cut the figure; the pockets can be measured and cut without a pattern.

The Storage Man

To make a storage man like the one shown here, you'll need:

heavy-weight denim, 36 inches wide, $3\frac{1}{8}$ yards.
unwoven interfacing—a piece 5 feet by 22 inches.
poster paper—the same amount as the interfacing (can be pieced).
contrast denim, white or cream colored—a piece $8\frac{1}{2}$ by $10\frac{1}{2}$ inches.
chalk; a ruler; 2 white badges; a large clip.

Begin by drawing the basic shape on the poster paper, using the dimensions shown on the cutting plan. The easiest way is to draw a line down the middle of the sheet, 11 inches from either side. This center line will help you to center the leg section and the head. If you have trouble drawing a circle, use a plate as a pattern. Cut out the paper shape, cutting slightly inside the line all around, and curving the corners. Place the shape on the fabric as shown in the cutting plan, and draw around it with the chalk. Draw the back facing in the same way. Cut out the pockets, following measurements on the diagram. Cut a duplicate shape from the interfacing.

Baste the interfacing to the wrong side of the basic shape. To make pockets: fold each pocket in half, crosswise, right sides together. Stitch around the three raw edges $\frac{1}{4}$ inch from the edge, leaving a gap of about 2 inches on one side. Trim the corners, turn the pocket right side out, and pull the corners with a strong needle to make them square. Press well, tucking under the raw edges.

Make a pleat along each side of the pocket by folding it $1\frac{1}{4}$ inches from the edge and bringing this folded edge to the finished edge of the pocket. Press the pleat well, using a damp cloth. On the center top and the leg section pockets, make two additional folds, facing each other, at the center. Pin the pocket in the appropriate position on the shape, placing the folded edge (as distinguished from the 3 stitched edges) toward the bottom. Pull the pleat fold out of the way along each side, but pin it down at the lower edge. Topstitch around the side and lower edges of the pocket. On the top center and leg section pockets, stitch vertically between the pleats.

Fold the loop strip in half lengthwise, right sides together, leaving a 2-inch gap on the long side. Trim the seam allowance at the corners, turn, and press. Close the opening in the seam by hand. Topstitch the strip to the shape at both ends, aligning it with the lower edge of the side pockets. Adjust and pin the loops into position. The loops are placed at intervals of $\frac{3}{8}$ of an inch. When you have positioned the loops, stitch them down.

Fold each strap in half lengthwise, right sides together, and stitch along the long edge. Turn the strap right side out, and topstitch along the side edges. Stitch one end under the top corner of the top pocket, and pin the other end at the shoulder.

Cut the contrast denim in half to make 2 pieces, $4\frac{1}{4}$ by $5\frac{1}{4}$ inches. Trim one corner of each piece to follow the curve at the "hand" position on the shape. Turn under $\frac{1}{4}$ inch all around, and press. Pin and topstitch each "hand" about $\frac{1}{2}$ inch in from the raw edge of the shape. Make 4 vertical lines of stitching with contrast thread to represent fingers.

Stitch the facing legs to the facing torso, and press the seam open. Zigzag stitch or hand overcast the opening. Lay the front shape on the facing, *right sides together*, pin, baste, and stitch around the edges, taking a $\frac{5}{8}$-inch seam allowance. Be careful not to catch in the pockets, but *do* catch in the upper ends of the straps. Trim the seam allowance to $\frac{1}{4}$ inch, clip the curves around head and hands, and turn the figure right side out. Press well, using a damp cloth or steam iron. Insert the paper shape.

To hang the storage man, drive a few nails through the head, shoulders, feet, and hands. Badges and a clip suggest eyes and mouth.

A Place to Play

Finding enough space for children's activities can be a problem, especially if two children must share a room. On these pages are a few ideas for making the most of limited space.

The bar and freezer baskets shown above are a practical way of storing toys and games without using valuable floor space. Toys are clearly visible, and so less likely to be mislaid. The work surface, cut from a length of plywood, was fastened to the wall with brackets.

Anglepoise lamps, clamped onto the edge, can be swiveled around to provide extra light for playing on the floor.

Bunk beds are popular with most children. The ingenious arrangement shown opposite (below) carries the bunk bed idea a step further, with both beds suspended from the ceiling, and toys stored on wide shelves to each side of the beds, leaving space below for large work tables.

On the following pages are two examples of multipurpose furniture: an old-fashioned wardrobe converted into a play-study corner, and a cylindrical free-standing closet that holds clothing, toys, and books.

If you're really bursting out of your home, you might consider converting part of your garage into a children's room—particularly if you have a big garage.

Left: designed for work and play—plenty of floor space and a large expanse of work table. Baskets slide along the bar, providing handy storage.

Right: the ever-popular bunk beds. The section in the middle gives added headroom, can be taken out if beds are separated.

Below: skilled carpentry and an ingenious plan for utilizing space near the ceiling converted a small room into a work, sleep, and play room for two young children.

Above and left: a corner of one's own. A large wardrobe was fitted with a work table, two swinging blackboard panels, pegs for toys, a shelf for books, a lamp, and a cozy nook for reading. Projecting blocks of wood give your child access to the upper level.

Above: a cylindrical, free-standing closet holds toys, books, and clothes. The wooden boxes hold toys, and are fun for small children to play games in.

Left: refinished on the inside, and painted bright yellow, a former garage makes an ideal playroom.

Three-in-one Room

When one large room has to serve as living room, dining room, and study, it may be difficult to get your furnishings organized into a pleasing and functional arrangement. The solution shown here is to put up a partial room divider which defines the dining area, and, on the other side, provides work space, storage space, and a place for the TV set. A tall bookcase helps to give the divider an "architectural" quality. (Don't forget that rows of colorfully bound books do wonders for the look of a room, quite apart from their intrinsic value.)

Drawer, work table, and cabinet units in laminated wood can be obtained from many furniture dealers. Alternatively, buy unfinished wood units, and stain or paint them yourself. Buy the wood for the wall to correspond to the width of the assembled units. Construction is simply a matter of a few uprights and several lengths of plywood. The plywood has been left bare, and serves effectively as a bulletin board. For a little more money, you could face it with cork tiles, to give a rich, warm look. On the dining alcove side, you can paint the wall to match the other walls, or call attention to it with wallpaper or printed or textured fabric.

If you have a great many books, you could use two bookcases back-to-back, with one of them facing the study area. Or you could use a wider bookcase, which would have the effect of giving a more enclosed feeling.

A room divider such as this is an especially good idea for a one-room apartment (unless the room is very small), for it creates the illusion of having more than one room. The smaller area could serve as either a dining or a sleeping alcove.

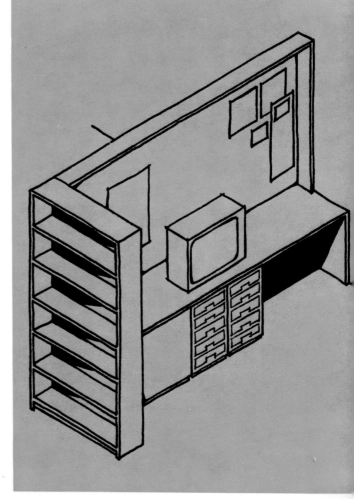

Above: the basic components of the divider, shown in this sketch, can be varied as desired.

Below: this floor plan shows the divider in relation to the rest of the room. The shaded area represents the view in the photograph opposite.

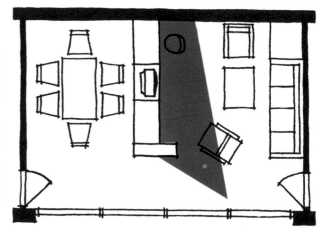

Lamps from Bottles

You can prolong the usefulness of handsome wine bottles by turning them into good-looking lamps, such as the ones shown here. Many wine bottles (and other bottles as well) have interesting shapes that lend themselves well to various decorating schemes. Liqueur bottles, such as those for Grand Marnier, Cointreau, and Benedictine, are a good choice, because they have squat shapes and are less likely to tip over than tall, narrow bottles. If you want to use a slender shape, choose your lampshade carefully to make sure it's in proportion to the base. To make the lamp steadier, you might fill the bottle with sand or pebbles.

The striking lamp second from right in the picture was made with a gallon jug filled with layers of beans, peas, and lentils. So as not to disturb the layers, the maker of the lamp used a socket with the cord coming out of the side, rather than down through the bottom.

For most lamps, you'll want to run the cord through the bottle to make it less conspicuous. To do this, fix the bottle securely on its side so that it won't slip or roll around. Drill a hole one inch up from the bottom, using a $\frac{1}{4}$-inch carbide tip drill at medium speed. Prepare the bottle for drilling by first sticking a small piece of putty, about $\frac{1}{4}$-inch thick, on the spot to be drilled, making a small dent in it, and filling the dent with turpentine. This will lubricate the drill.

When you go to buy hardware for the lamp, take the bottle with you, so as to be sure to get the correct size.

For lamps constructed with the cord to one side, it's advisable to use a harp and finial; this will support the shade independently of the bulb and socket.

Left: ceramic *vin rosé* crocks were used for the attractive pair of lamps at far left. A gallon jug filled with beans, peas, and lentils, and a half-gallon sherry bottle were used to make the other two lamps.

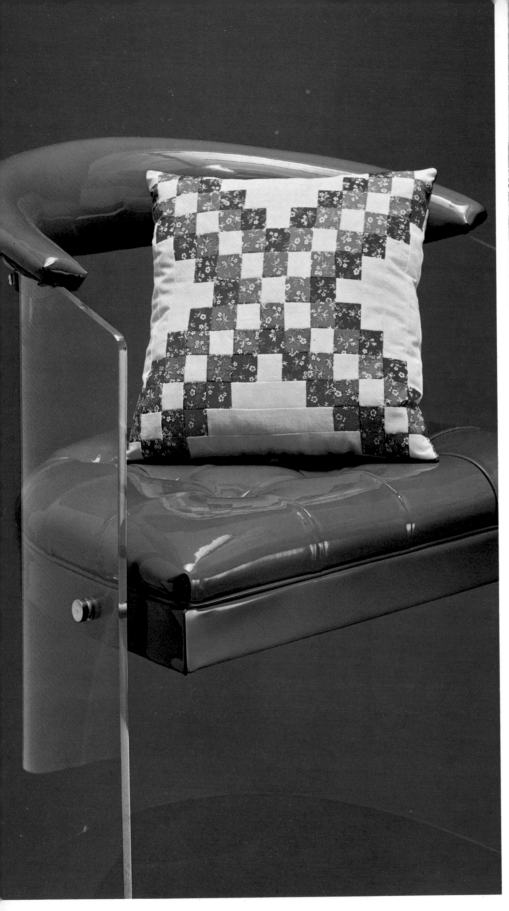

Left: one of the most popular patchwork designs, Triple Irish Chain is shown here used for a bright red, white, and blue pillow. Directions for making the pillow are given on these pages.

Above: another pillow using the Pineapple pattern, decorates an occasional chair. On the wall is a framed block of Crown of Thorns.

Above right: a *tour de force* for an experienced patchworker, the Star of Bethlehem pattern is here appliquéd to a bedspread.

Pretty Patchwork

Blue printed cotton fabric—3 inches of 36-inch fabric, or any size piece that will yield forty-four $1\frac{1}{2}$-inch squares.
Red printed cotton fabric—3 inches of 36-inch fabric (enough for thirty-six $1\frac{1}{2}$-inch squares).
stuffing material, such as kapok. (optional)
some thin *cardboard*.

A traditional American craft, patchwork is enjoying a revival of popularity. Its pleasing geometric patterns live well with many different decorating styles.

On these pages we give directions for making the simple and attractive Triple Irish Chain pillow cover shown opposite.

Materials for the scatter pillow are:
White cotton fabric (plain, close weave)—$\frac{1}{2}$ yard of 36-inch fabric.

For the finished item to look good, patchwork pieces must be seamed together precisely. The sizes given below include a $\frac{1}{4}$-inch seam allowance. If you're unsure of your ability to maintain an even seam allowance, it's a good idea to cut cardboard patterns of the *finished* size of each patch. Cut a cardboard strip measuring 7 inches by 1 inch, another 5 by 1, another 3 by 1, and a 1-inch square. Lay the pattern on the wrong side of the cloth and draw around the edge with a pencil. Be sure to align the pattern with the straight grain of the fabric. Allow at least $\frac{1}{2}$-inch between one drawn patch and the next. Cut out the fabric patches, cutting $\frac{1}{4}$-inch outside the penciled lines. In joining patches, match the penciled stitching lines carefully. Press seams to one side or another, not open.

Cut a piece $13\frac{1}{2}$ inches square from the white fabric. This will be the back of the pillow. From the remaining white fabric, cut: 4 strips measuring $1\frac{1}{2}$ inches by $7\frac{1}{2}$ inches; 4 strips $1\frac{1}{2}$ by $5\frac{1}{2}$; 4 strips $1\frac{1}{2}$ by $3\frac{1}{2}$; and twenty-nine $1\frac{1}{2}$-inch squares.

From the blue fabric cut forty-four $1\frac{1}{2}$-inch squares, and from the red cut 36 squares of $1\frac{1}{2}$-inches each.

Begin joining the patches, following the diagram shown at left. Seam 3 and 4 to 2; then seam this strip to 1. Seam 6, 7, 5, 8, and 9 together; then seam this strip to the 3-2-4 strip. Continue adding strips and patches, using the photograph as a guide for placement. When your $13\frac{1}{2}$-inch block is complete, press it well, and seam it to the plain square, placing right sides together and taking a $\frac{1}{4}$-inch seam allowance all around. Leave an 8-inch gap along one side. Stuff the pillow, and close the gap firmly with small stitches.

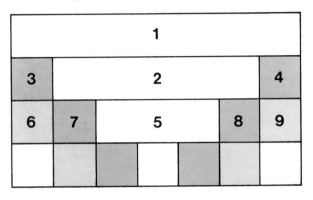

Above: this shows the suggested order of joining the squares, and corresponds to the center section (top four rows) on the photograph.

Right: complete block showing the correct position of the squares.

Decorate with Crochet

If you've discovered the fun of crocheting, you can turn a plain lampshade into an eye-catching accessory. If you don't yet know how to crochet, get a simple instruction book, or ask a friend to show you how. Crochet is easy to learn—much easier than knitting—and you can do it while watching TV.

The crochet borders of this lampshade cover are joined with a simple knotted lattice.

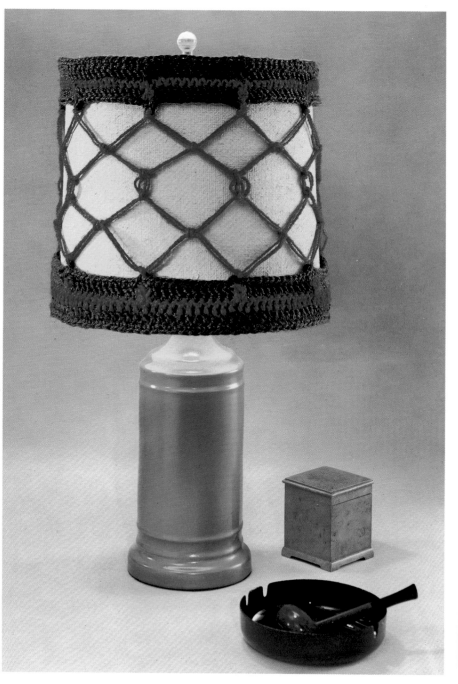

A handsome accessory for a study or a boy's room, this lampshade is crocheted with jute fiber to resemble a drum.

Below: a detail of the work shows the lark's head knot joined to the picot made in the red band, and the square knots forming the lattice.

The pattern can be made to fit any medium-sized drum-shaped shade. On these pages are directions for making the shade cover, plus some more elaborate designs you could adapt.

To make the shade cover you will need: one 4-oz spool of bright red *jute cord*. one 4-oz. spool of royal blue *jute cord*. *A crochet hook*, size F (Canadian size 10 or I.S.R. size 4.00), or whatever size will give you the correct gauge: 3 dc (see note) to 1 inch.

To work the top band: starting at top edge with blue, crochet a chain long enough to fit comfortably around top of shade. 1*st row (wrong side):* sc in 2nd ch from hook and in each ch across; ch 3; turn. 2*nd row:* skip first sc; dc in each sc across. With markers divide last row into 9 sections as evenly spaced as possible. Leave only *half* a space at each end, as these will be joined together to make one space. Break off blue, attach red and ch 1, turn. 3*rd row:* with red, sc in each dc to first marker; *sc in marked dc; ch 4; sc in 4th ch from hook (picot made); sc in each dc to next marker. Repeat from * across, ending in pattern. Break off red; attach blue; ch 3 and turn. 4*th row:* with blue, dc in each sc to

first picot; * work 2 sl sts in top of picot; dc in each sc to next picot. Repeat from * across, ending in pattern. Break off yarn.

To work the bottom band: starting at lower edge with blue, crochet a chain long enough to fit comfortably around lower edge of shade. 1*st row (right side):* dc in 4th ch from hook and in each ch across. Break off blue; attach red and ch 3; turn. Divide into 9 sections as before. 2*nd row:* with red, dc in each dc to first marker; * dc in marked dc; ch 5; sc in 5th ch from hook (picot); dc in each dc to next marker. Repeat from * across, ending in pattern. Break off red; attach blue and ch 3; turn. 3*rd row:* repeat 4th row of top band working into dc's instead of sc's. Break off. With right side facing you, and with blue, work a row of sc across both long edges of band.

To make up: with wrong side facing you, whipstitch ends of top band together to form a circle. Repeat with bottom band.

Slip top and bottom bands in position over shade. Cut 9 double lengths of red jute, each double length measuring 6 times the distance from bottom edge of top band to top edge of bottom band. 1*st knot row:* fold a double strand of jute in half. Draw folded end

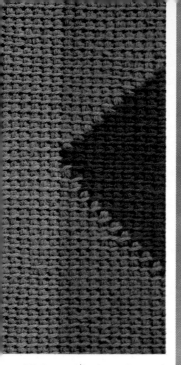

Right: a blanket trimmed with brilliant triangles of color, crocheted in an afghan stitch (detail shown above), makes a dramatic bedspread. Deep fringe, and a matching pillow cover with tassels, complete the effect.

Left: a fancy pattern—done in a simple stitch, single crochet—makes a lovely chair seat cover for a traditional room.

through blue st at end of a picot on bottom edge of top band. Draw ends through loop and pull tightly to make a lark's head knot. Repeat on the remaining picots around the edge of the top band. *2nd knot row:* take a double strand from one knot, and a double strand from the next knot, and make a square knot, joining the strands approximately 2 inches from each picot. The actual measurement will vary with the size of the work, but the strands should form an angle to the band similar to that shown in the photo. (To make a square knot, cross right strand over left and draw end through loop; cross left strand over right and draw end through loop; tighten.)

Make 8 more square knots around shade. *3rd knot row:* following photograph for placement, work a square knot about 2 inches below last row of knots, then work a second square knot directly under it, leaving a small space between knots as shown (double knot made). Continue around in this manner, making 8 more double knots. *4th knot row:* work as for first knot row, making square knots 2 inches from last row. *5th knot row:* tie a square knot in each st directly above each picot on bottom band.

Note—abbreviations: dc=double crochet (English treble); sc=single crochet (English double); ch=chain; sl st=slip stitch.

Questions & Answers

One fascinating aspect of decorating is its amazing variety. No two situations are alike. Even though whole housing developments and apartment buildings may consist of virtually identical dwellings, the needs and tastes of each family will inevitably call for different decorating styles. In fact, one of the challenges of modern decorating is to create uniquely personal surroundings within the framework of impersonal and similar houses or apartments. It can be done, though. Manufacturers of furniture, carpets wall coverings, paints, and all the other household furnishings, have developed an enormous range of products to meet every taste and budget.

People in older houses have a different set of challenges than dwellers in modern homes. They are faced with how to turn wasted space into useful space, how to liven up tired looking walls and floors, and how to disguise architectural oddities.

Few of us can afford to hire a professional decorator and give him or her a free hand. Moreover, there's usually more satisfaction in working out your own decorating solutions. Still, you can often profit from other people's experiences. Some of the questions and answers that follow in the next few pages may well relate to your own decorating problems. They cover a wide range of situations, from a "bowling alley" living room to an aggressive chartreuse carpet. The questions are grouped under four headings: "Managing Space," "Tricks and Transformations," "Practical Matters," and "Shopping Sense." This last category includes some guidelines you can apply in buying wooden and upholstered furniture. Finally, a detailed chart on the bewildering variety of man-made fabrics available today, their special characteristics, and their care, will help you buy fabrics wisely.

Even if the questions don't pertain exactly to your special decorating problems, the answers may well stimulate you to come up with your own decorating innovations. In any case, they'll show you the wealth of possibilities open to the amateur decorator.

Saving money in decorating often means doing it yourself—whether it is wood paneling, lined draperies, or wallpaper. With a good instruction book, you can learn all kinds of useful techniques.

Managing Space

Our dining room is an L off the living room, but I'd like to make it seem more like a separate room. The living room walls are white. Would it be a good idea to paper the walls of the alcove in a pattern?

Yes, that would be a good way to achieve a feeling of separateness between the two areas. The only potential problem is the line where the dining alcove paper meets the living room paper along the bottom of the L. If there is a structural break here—a jog or a projecting support—the change of paper will appear natural, as it will on the inside corner of the L, where the wall makes a right angle. But if the long wall is unbroken, the join could look awkward, depending on the paper you choose. A paper that contrasts markedly with your living room walls would be preferable to one that has a pale background, especially a white or off-white one. In the latter case, the inevitable split motifs at the edge would appear to be floating uncomfortably in a sort of visual no man's land. If you plan to use paper with a pale background in the L, you should place a tall piece of furniture, or a narrow room divider at the meeting point to make the break seem more decisive. Even some open shelves, placed at right angles to the wall, would do the trick. The change of wall covering would still be visible, but the shelves and the objects on them would distract the eye sufficiently to make the join inconspicuous. Whatever paper you choose, make sure that the edge of the join is absolutely vertical.

My living room is a "bowling alley"— 20 feet long and only 9 feet wide. Is there any cheap way to make it appear wider?

Yes, there are several cheap ways to make it appear wider. For example, you can re-decorate one or both of the short end walls, using a darker or brighter color paint than you have on the other walls, or papering one wall with an interesting pattern. (Don't overlook scenic, "fool the eye" patterns.)

Large mirrors are expensive, but mirror tiles are cheap, and can serve the same purpose. You could cover part of one long wall with these tiles (easy for an amateur decorator to attach) to help widen the room. A good place to put them would be right next to the redecorated end wall, so that the effect would be apparently extended.

Placement of furniture can affect the apparent shape of a room. By placing a sofa along one of the short walls you can emphasize, and seemingly widen, that wall. If you have a rather long sofa, you may have no alternative to placing it on a long wall, but you can balance it with long, low bookshelves along an adjacent short wall. A desk placed at right angles to the long wall would help to break up the length of the room. You might even set aside part of the room as a study area, using a fretwork panel or a bead curtain as a room divider. These are fairly cheap and easy to install. What's more, they achieve the desired visual break with a minimum of bulk, and without significantly reducing the light passing from one area to the next. To emphasize the break, you could paint or paper this corner to contrast with the rest of the long wall.

Window treatments are always important in "shaping" a wall. Without knowing the locations and sizes of your windows, it's difficult to advise a specific treatment. However, in general it's a good idea to treat a window in a short wall in such a way as to accentuate the horizontal: for example, draw draperies covering the whole width of the wall. Unless the ceiling is low, a valance or cornice is a good addition to this window treatment. Windows in the long wall should be emphasized with curtains, draperies, or blinds that contrast noticeably with the surrounding wall area. This will help to break up the long expanse of wall. However, avoid dramatizing such windows at the expense of the short walls. You don't want them to retreat into obscurity.

I've inherited a four-poster bed. It's beautiful, but it overwhelms our tiny bedroom. How can I make it look less out-of-proportion?

Lucky you! Few people today own such a distinctive piece of furniture. Still, it can be something of a problem in a small room. There are several ways to minimize the size of the bed, depending on your decorating scheme. A sheer lace or net canopy will give an airy look, which is particularly effective on an arched frame. The traditional covering for the bed itself is a white candlewick bedspread. If your room is decorated in pale colors, you may decide that this simple treatment will be the best one.

A bolder approach would be to cover the bed and the walls with the same allover print—either fabric and matching paper, or fabric for walls as well. The colors in the print should harmonize closely with the color of the carpet. (Wall-to-wall carpet, incidentally, will help the room appear larger). You can also use a plain version of this allover treatment, using solid colors or a subtle stripe. Again, a sheer canopy in a harmonizing color will keep the top of the bed from being obtrusive. You might also consider painting or papering your ceiling to match.

If you decide on a solid color treatment for the room, add a group of pictures, or some framed needlework, to the area above the headboard. This will attract the eye *past* the outer posts (which, along with the canopy, are what make the bed seem too large for the room). Another trick is to curtain the wall-side posts with a solid color matching the walls, and line the curtain with a print or stripe. This is another way of drawing attention to the head of the bed.

My husband and I live in a large studio apartment (see enclosed plan), which we'd like to divide into living room and bedroom. We'd rather have the living area at the window end, next to the kitchen. On the other hand, having the main entrance in the bedroom seems a bit back to front. Also, we don't want to cut off the morning sunlight. Can you suggest a solution to the dilemna?

"See-through" is the kind of solution you need here. What you want is room dividers that don't completely cut off part of the room, but at the same time tend to stop the eye from looking farther.

The diagram below illustrates a room divider of the cabinet-bookshelf type (see the photo on page 70,) which is a useful furnishing for the living room. You can adjust the amount of sunlight you get in the bedroom by filling the shelves as full or as sparsely as you like. A low chest of drawers behind the shelves on the bedroom side will be invisible from the living room.

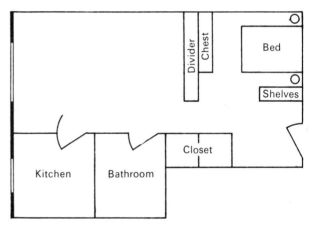

To partially screen the bed from the entrance area, we suggest a tall stack of open shelves (an *étagère*) on which you can place accessories and any plants that thrive away from direct sunlight. This won't completely screen off the bed, but will tend to call attention to itself, and will also create the effect of a separate entrance hall.

The resulting sleeping area won't be very large, so we suggest flanking the bed with two hanging lamps instead of end tables with lamps.

Once you have made yourself an entrance hall, make it an interesting one. You might put some bright wallpaper and a mirror on the short wall immediately opposite the door. A small table holding a large vase filled with big paper poppies, or an old-fashioned coat rack painted a bright color would also add interest to what might otherwise be a rather dead corner of your apartment.

Tricks and Transformations

I thought a bright roller blind over my kitchen window would add a bit of pattern to the room, but I forgot it would be rolled up most of the time I'm using the kitchen. I had it especially made, so it wasn't any bargain. What can I do with it now? The room still needs brightening.

If you can still get the material, why not make some matching curtains—either plain or café type? A harmonizing solid color would be most attractive. If a curtain seems too fussy in that location, use a piece of the fabric as a wall hanging. Attach some plain braid along the top, and a row of ball fringe at the bottom. Attach a narrow strip of wood to the upper edge on the back, and run a string from one corner to the other. Hang it by the string.

You could also paint the window frame and the other woodwork in the kitchen to match or contrast with the blind fabric.

Here's an idea for a really custom-decorated effect: a stencil design for your cabinets. Trace a motif from the blind fabric. Then lay the tracing paper over some carbon paper on top of a piece of thin cardboard. Transfer the design onto the cardboard, and cut it out. Using gloss paint in an appropriate color, stencil the design onto your cabinets (first marking the locations of the motifs with a pencil).

There are lots of other ways to brighten a kitchen: a piece of painted pegboard hung with copper pans and molds; a colorful hanging lamp; a pretty wall calendar; gaily printed tea towels; plants and flowers.

Whoever built our apartment managed to put overhead fixture outlets in the most awkward location. For example, one of them is not only off-center but also right over the door, thus ruling out low-hanging fixtures. Any suggestions? Well placed, a ceiling light fixture can be a handsome addition to a room. Badly placed, it can be an irritation.

Consider each room separately. Is there a real need for an overhead light in that room? In a kitchen, you do need one for diffused lighting, and it should be placed high, so there's no real problem. An entrance hall, too, should probably have an overhead light. If a low-hanging fixture isn't feasible in your hall, choose a fixture that's reasonably attractive and unobtrusive, and that will diffuse the light gently. Supplement this with a small but eye-catching table lamp that will give the desired warm glow. If you make this lamp part of an attractive grouping —say a telephone table, bench, and mirror, you can effectively draw attention to this part of the hall, so that the overhead light merely serves as a part of the background.

Most living rooms and bedrooms don't really need an overhead light, provided they have enough other light fixtures. Good-sized table lamps—particularly if some or all of them have pale translucent shades—can provide all the light you need in a living room or bedroom. You can cover the overhead outlet with contact paper, paint it to match the ceiling, and forget about it. If you like, you can augment the lamps with strip lighting behind a window cornice, or with a pair of wall sconces.

The dining room is a bit trickier. You really do need light for the whole table. First of all, see if there is any way to arrange the furniture so that it lines up with the outlet. The table needn't be smack in the center of the room. If you can't rearrange the furniture, your most attractive option is to use wall sconces and/or table lamps to light the room and your dining table. Use different kinds of candles and holders to vary the effect—from cozy and informal to festive and elegant.

We have the dreariest bathroom in the world: old discolored white tiles, a prewar bathtub, exposed pipes. Any ideas for making it more attractive?
First of all, a beauty treatment for that aging tile: clean it by applying laundry starch, and then going over it with a soft cloth. A sponge dipped in a solution of ammonia and water will give the tile an extra sparkle. A good treatment for water rust stains is to rub the stain with borax sprinkled with lemon juice.

Now for more positive action. The extent of the transformation will depend somewhat on whether you own your house or rent it. In the latter case, the landlord might object to some additions and alterations.

In any case, you can probably paint the nontiled areas of the wall and the ceiling. Paint these surfaces a vivid color, stripes, or a mural. If you're not clever with a brush, use a vinyl wall covering instead. Cover the ceiling, too. Paint those exposed pipes with your chosen color where they run along the painted or papered wall, and paint them white where they run along the tile.

Continue the color, while adding a luxurious texture, with nylon bathroom carpeting. It's cheap, it's easy to cut and fit yourself, and it's washable. It will also make the room appear larger, and will cover any dismal patches on the floor.

If you have a small, mirrored medicine cabinet over the basin, consider getting rid of it. Substitute a good quality mirror with a pretty frame, perhaps an oval one. Attach a couple of wall lamps on either side. Put the medicines in a small box (with a lock, if you have children) and stow it in a drawer, in a larger cabinet—which you've painted a bright color, of course—or in your bathroom closet, if you have one. Some of your cosmetics probably come in decorative bottles and jars. Leave them out on display. The top of the aforementioned cabinet should do nicely. Less decorative items can be put away, or better still, decanted into attractive bottles you've picked up here and there. You can make these bottles even more attractive with a special paint suited to glass, which you can buy in a hobby shop.

If the bathroom is large enough, add a stool or a small wicker chair with a colorful cushion. This will give you a pleasant place to sit while giving yourself a manicure, or drying your hair. Add a magazine rack and some magazines for reading in the tub.

If there's an overhead lighting outlet, use a low-hanging basket shade or one of the turn-of-the-century style shades with fringe. A tinted bulb, plus the colored shade, will cast a warm glow on that cold white tile.

A new shower curtain might give the room a lift. If you can't find just what you want in the stores, buy a plain plastic curtain to serve as a liner, and make your own outer curtain with whatever fabric you like. (Don't however, use chintz, because it loses its distinctive finish in damp surroundings.)

Use contact paper, or some of your wallpaper, to cover a plain wastebasket.

If you're handy at carpentry, or don't mind paying a carpenter to do this one job, you can encase that old tub in a new outer shell, which you can tile. This will not only make your bathroom prettier, but, depending on the size of the surface area surrounding the tub, will also give you space for putting bath accessories and plants.

The master bedroom in our 120-year-old house has a fireplace that is brick with a wooden mantel. We don't use it, and we can't afford to get rid of it. How can we incorporate it into our modern decorating scheme?
Once you get the fireplace thoroughly cleaned and the chimney closed, you have a number of alternative treatments from which to choose.

If the brickwork is attractive, you could leave it as it is, perhaps just painting the mantel to blend in with the walls. If you really want to minimize the shape of the fireplace, your best bet is to paint the brickwork also, the same inside and out.

If you like the fresh green look of plants, fill the fireplace cavity with masses of them—ferns, grape ivy, African violets—or use just one big plant, such as a Mexican breadfruit. For added interest, attach mirror tiles to the back of the fireplace. You get twice the plants for the same amount of care.

You could try using your fireplace as a rather special frame for a modern picture. Or, if you're handy with a needle, make a modern version of an old-fashioned fire screen. Copy a favorite abstract painting, transfer it to a piece of strong linen or cotton, and embroider it with needlepoint, or appliqué an abstract design onto it. Stretch the completed embroidery or appliqué on a wooden frame, and attach it to any suitable pedestal or stand, or hang it from the brickwork with picture wire.

You can also put a couple of shelves in the fireplace for displaying a few treasured objects, or just for books.

My husband has insisted on buying an enormous black imitation leather chair, which is jarring with my lemon yellow French provincial decor. Short of putting a screen around it, what can I do to make it less aggressive?
This may sound heartless, but you should learn to live with it. A home is for comfort, and if the chair helps your husband unwind at the end of the day, it's worth sacrificing your homogeneous decorating scheme.

Fortunately, there are many ways to adapt the room so that the decor, in a sense, embraces the chair. (Remember what results when an oyster is irritated by a grain of sand!) Don't be afraid to adulterate your French provincial still further. If you can afford to buy another piece of furniture, make it a sleek modern item: for example, a black painted cabinet with glass doors. If you've still got some money left over, buy a large abstract lithograph, frame it, and hang it above the cabinet. This grouping might steal some of the attention away from the monster chair.

Sit down with a stack of decorating magazines, and go through them thoughtfully. You'll find dozens of rooms happily combining traditional and modern styles, one of which may give you an idea that you can adapt to your own surroundings.

Finally consider rearranging your living room (assuming it's a reasonable size) so that your French-style furniture occupies most of the area, with the remainder—separated with a suitable room divider—devoted to homey comfort. Your living room may be more flexible than you think.

The walls in our house are hopelessly cracked and irregular. A new paint job won't help, and neither, I suspect, will wallpaper. We can't afford paneling. Any suitable alternative?
You have a variety of solutions at your disposal. One of them, or a combination of two or more, should do the trick.

There is a kind of wallpaper, called "chip-paper," that will disguise your walls. It consists of two layers of paper glued together with tiny chips of wood between them. Hang the paper as you would any wallpaper, and paint it whatever color you like. You'll be surprised how effectively it conceals the most depressing patches of your walls—and ceilings, too.

Many of the new vinyl wall coverings will cover cracks and other blemishes well. The bolder and brighter the pattern, the better the disguise.

If a wall is in terrible condition, your best bet is fabric stretched over battens attached to the wall at ceiling and floor. A few vertical battens will help to anchor the fabric, and will also come in handy when you want to hang a picture.

Pictures, by the way, can often serve to conceal minor defects in a wall. Of course, you can't put a picture just anywhere, but a few large ones, judiciously placed, may serve the purpose.

If you need more shelf space—and who doesn't?—you can kill two birds with one stone by covering an unsightly wall with shelves. Buy unpainted planks and paint them yourself. If the wall is structurally sound, attach the shelves to it with metal strips and brackets. If the wall seems a bit insecure, you'd better choose freestanding bookshelves. Once filled with books and decorative objects, the shelves will hide your problem walls.

We've bought the living room and dining room carpeting left by the previous tenant. The price was reasonable, but the colour is a glaring chartreuse. We don't want to buy more chartreuse furnishings, but we can't ignore the carpets in planning our color scheme. What can we do?

There are basically two approaches you can use: the bold and the conciliatory. The bold approach would be to counter the chartreuse with an equally intense complementary color —for example, a rich purple—which would balance the green and make it look an intentional choice. If you're very brave, you might even paint the walls purple; or paint one wall purple and the rest off-white. Use printed draperies combining the two colors. Natural wood tones will mellow the effect; white painted furniture will cool it; black paint and stainless steel will give additional drama.

The conciliatory approach would be to surround the green with related hues, such as lemon yellow or turquoise, or with a lot of white. Some paler and darker greens would also help to integrate the bright chartreuse.

If the carpet is a plain, short pile, you might add an inexpensive shaggy area rug to cut down the large expanse of chartreuse. A fake fur rug would achieve a similar effect more luxuriously.

Remember that once you've acquired some pictures, lamps, and other accessories to attract the eye, your carpet won't seem nearly so glaring to you as it does now.

The rooms of our apartment are connected by a long, dark hallway, now painted hospital green. How can we make it more attractive?

Why not break up that long expanse with decorative panels? Select some wallpaper or contact paper in an allover pattern (see the door project, pages 96-99), and some decorative molding strips to go around the edges of each patterned area. You will need to do some careful planning first, deciding on the height and width of the panels, and their location on the wall. You might decide to confine them to one side of the hallway— particularly if the hall is rather narrow, and the doors located in such a way that placing the panels directly opposite one another would be difficult. A chair rail, or dado, running beneath the panels, would give a feeling of unity to the grouping.

A similar treatment, and one better suited to a modern interior, would be to paper the entire hallway with a pattern that's light and bright, then paint the doors and surrounding woodwork a contrasting color.

Some wall coverings have shiny surfaces that reflect light. One of these might be the ideal solution if getting enough light in the hallway is difficult. If overhead fixtures are missing or inadequate, add a wall or table lamp. In fact, an excellent way to interrupt a monotonous stretch of hallway is with a small table—such as a console table—a lamp, and a picture or mirror. Such a grouping should be placed near an architectural feature, such as a door or an arch, to give it something to relate to. A few fresh flowers on the table will do wonders to brighten up the hall.

You can add a lot of interest to a hallway by using it to display a favorite collection. Wood carvings, teacups, fossils, or whatever you collect could make a fascinating display either on open shelves or in cabinets. But don't let the collection languish in the dark. Use spotlights and other direct lighting to make the most of your treasures.

Practical Matters

Our dining room is a glorified corridor to the rest of the house, and the carpet is beginning to show signs of wear. I've been thinking of carpet tiles as a solution. What are the advantages and disadvantages?

Carpet tiles would probably be a very good solution to your "thruway" dining room. You can move them around to distribute wear, and you can lay them yourself, thus saving the installation cost. They're relatively inexpensive, compared to regular carpeting, though the better looking varieties can be as expensive as carpeting.

The disadvantages are, first, that the joins will show to some extent, depending on the type and quality of the tile, and, second, that you have considerably less choice in textures and colors. However, in a dining room neither of these drawbacks is as significant as it would be in a living room, where the floor is a more important part of the decorating scheme. Most dining rooms are pretty well filled with table and chairs, and possibly a sideboard as well. The floor is relatively inconspicuous. If you choose carpet tiles in an unobtrusive color, you should find them a satisfactory solution.

Before you buy carpet tiles, however, give a thought to the possibility of vinyl tiles or sheet vinyl. This is very hard wearing, and is available in a wide range of colors and patterns.

We have three girls in their teens, and I am expecting again. The only suitable room for the baby is directly over the family room, which seems permanently full of noisy teenagers. What can I do in the way of soundproofing so that neither baby nor girls suffer?

You can buy special acoustical tiles to apply to the ceiling of the family room. Adhesive-backed cork tiles, which are a handsome wall treatment, will also reduce reverberations. For the floor in the baby's room, wall-to-wall carpeting is a must. You can get by with cheap carpeting and, of course, it should be easily cleaned. Nylon carpeting, or carpet tiles, would be a good choice. A polyurethane underlay is a good sound insulator, and is nonflammable. Acoustic tiles for the nursery ceiling would also be a good idea.

The more soft furnishings you have in a room, the more sound absorbent it will be. Curtains, cushions, and rugs can all help. If the family room now has a hard-surface flooring, consider buying an inexpensive room-size rug, perhaps a piece of cord broadloom. This wears like iron, even when danced on.

You can't ask the teens to give up their music, but insist that it is played at a reasonable level. Besides irritating Baby upstairs, extremely loud music can actually impair the hearing of those in the room.

We have a corner lot, and our bedroom windows face the street. I hate net curtains, but I feel the room is a goldfish bowl. What can I do for some privacy during the day?

You have several alternatives that will give both sunlight and privacy. For a cheery informal look at low cost, café curtains are ideal. They'll screen the lower half of the window. Most café curtains cover only the lower half of the window; but you can buy, or make, two tier cafés for total coverage when you want it. If you choose one-tier curtains, add a roller blind in a harmonizing color print. You can trim the shade with braid to match the curtains, or cover it with the same fabric. Instead of a shade, you can use a plain venetian blind—preferably a modern one with narrow slats.

For a sleek modern look, vertical blinds (see the photo on page 53) are the answer. These are stiffened strips of fabric that operate on the same principal as Venetian blinds, only sideways. They can be adjusted to give total visibility, total privacy, and all gradations in between. Another advantage is that they give an illusion of extra height—a welcome bonus for modern low-ceilinged rooms.

Louvered shutters, though relatively expensive, are a charming treatment for windows in a traditional style room. With the lower shutters closed and the upper ones open, you have the best of both worlds.

Finally, don't overlook the possibilities of textured sheer curtains. All kinds of lovely and novel sheer woven fabrics are covering windows these days, and they're made in luscious colors. Pleated or gathered fully, these curtains will give all the privacy you need during the day. Add a roller blind for complete privacy at night.

We own several small Oriental rugs, which look lovely on our tile floors; but since my invalid mother has come to live with us, I worry about the possibility of her slipping on them. Is there any way to keep such rugs stationary?
A rubber bathmat placed under the rug will keep it from slipping around. If the rugs are considerably larger than bathmat-size, you could buy some thin sponge rubber carpet underlay, cut to the proper sizes. To be on the safe side, don't place a rug at the head of a stairway. This is sound advice for any home, irrespective of the age and physical condition of the occupants.

Shopping Sense

We're complete beginners in furniture shopping. Can you give us some tips to help us evaluate the quality of a piece of wood furniture? Should we avoid veneers, for example?
First of all, you can relax about veneers. Some of the finest furniture made today (and in the past) is veneered. Modern techniques make it possible to construct veneers that are very strong, as well as beautiful.

Whether the piece is veneered or solid, you should carefully inspect the *finish*. Is the grain of the wood attractive? Do the various surfaces blend in their color and grain? Is the finish smooth to the touch, even along the edges and inside drawers? Is the piece free from streaks, and deposits of varnish in recesses and corners?

Check for sturdiness of *construction*. Any table or chair that will be subjected to much stress should have corner block construction where the legs are joined; that is, there should be a diagonal piece of wood bracing the two adjacent sides. The underside of a chair seat should have several supporting ribs. Drawer corners should be joined with dovetailing, or at least with a tongue and groove, and not just nailed or glued together. There should be dust panels between drawers, and a center track or side glides so that drawers will slide in and out easily. Drawer pulls should be fastened through the wood, and not just attached to the outer surface. Cabinet doors should swing easily, and catch securely when closed.

Give thoughtful consideration to the *usefulness* of the item. If it's an end table, make sure it's the right height for your sofa. Check a dining table and chairs to make sure you have at least seven inches of knee clearance between them. Also check the clearance for the chair arms, if any. Obviously, you should sit on a chair to see if it's comfortable. If you are planning to place a desk or cabinet at a right angle to the wall, it should have a finished back.

What should we look for when buying a piece of upholstered furniture?
Upholstered furniture is more difficult to examine than wood furniture, because so many of the things that go into it can't be seen. You should rely heavily on the label stating the materials, and the proportion of each, used in the cushioning. Also, most reputable manufacturers will provide a description of the item's construction, and some kind of guarantee. Read this carefully.

The frame should be of hardwood such as ash, birch, or hard maple. If the piece has an exposed frame, check the legs for corner block reinforcement. Feel the upholstery carefully to see that it is smooth and well-padded, with no lumps. Feel the underside of the seat. You should be able to detect good strong webbing, covered with strong fabric. If the webbing is fabric, rather than steel or nylon, it should have no gaps.

Good quality upholstered pieces will have coil springs (except in modern, slimline furniture, which has flat "S" springs), and there should be at least eight of these to each seat, preferably hand-tied. Here again, you must rely on the manufacturer's statement and guarantee. Poor coil construction will have your chair or sofa looking and feeling saggy in a short time. You should also get written assurance that the filling material is moth-proofed, and, if your area is humid, resistant to mildew.

The body of a moderate priced upholstered piece is likely to be filled with cotton felt, or with a mixture of felt and shredded latex, hair, or polyester. Cotton padding or polyester fiber fill provides a smooth surface between the filling and the upholstery fabric.

The filling used in cushions is generally either foam rubber (latex) or polyurethane foam. The latter is in some ways preferable; it is mildew- and flame-resistant. The important factor—whether a cushion is latex or polyurethane—is its density. Lift the cushion. It should be fairly heavy. If it's lightweight, that means that the filling has low density, and will tend to collapse after a short time. Expensive furniture often has cushions filled with down, or with a combination of feathers and down. The only drawback to this kind of filling is that it can lose its plumpness after a few years. It's also a bad choice if one is allergic to feathers, but it gives a chair a luxurious look, and extra comfort.

If you're buying a chair or sofa that must stand up to heavy wear, you should look for: loose cushions, which can be turned to distribute wear (rather than a "tight back" piece—see example, page 43), and sturdy, closely woven fabric. These qualities, plus good solid construction, will ensure years of good wear.

Should I resist the temptation to buy the cream colored sofa I've fallen in love with? Do the new fabric-protecting sprays really work?
Unless you have small children or pets, you can relax and get your cream colored sofa. If the fabric isn't already protected with a stain-resistant finish, you should treat it thoroughly with one of the aerosol sprays recommended for this purpose. Yes, they do work astonishingly well. Remember, though, you should renew the treatment each time the sofa is cleaned. If you give the sofa reasonable care, it should look good for several years. When and if it begins to look a little dreary, you can slipcover it.

Opposite: shopping for furnishing fabrics can be a puzzle because of the many trademark names for man-made fibers. By describing what each fiber is like, and by listing its various brand names, this chart will help you understand what you're buying.

Man-made Fibers

Federal Trade Commission's Generic Names	Trademark Names	Some Principal Uses in Home Furnishings	Characteristics	General Care Instructions
RAYON (First produced in the USA in 1910)	Avicolor Aviloc Avisco Beau-Grip Briglo Coloray Comiso Dy-Lok Englo Enkrome Fibro Fibro DD Fibro FR Hi-Narco I.T. Jetspun Kolorbon Narco Narcon Ondelette Purilon Rayflex Skybloom Skyloft Softglo Strawn Super Narco Super Rayflex Suprenka Suprenka Hi Mod Tyron Tyweld Villwyte	Draperies Slipcovers Curtains Upholstery Tablecloths Sheets Bedspreads Blankets Floor coverings	Strong when dry. Highly absorbent. Soft and comfortable. Dyes easily. Takes all colors. Drapes well. Wrinkles easily. Weak when wet, and may shrink in laundering unless a finish is added to prevent this.	Some rayon fabrics must be dry cleaned, but others may be washed. If you wash rayon, use mild lukewarm water for both washing and rinsing. Iron while damp on the wrong side at a moderate setting. If you must iron on the right side, use a press cloth.
HIGH MODULUS RAYON	Avril Fiber 24 Fiber 40 Fiber 700 Nupron Xena Zantrel Zantrel 700	Mostly used in blends to add strength, and a soft silky hand ("feel")	Strong even when wet.	Same as rayon.
ANIDEX (First produced in the USA in 1970)	Anim/8	Upholstery Slipcovers	Imparts permanent stretch and recovery properties. Improves fit and appearance in home furnishing fabrics. Fabrics have no "rubbery" feeling. Resistant to gas fading, oxidation, sunlight, oils, and chlorine bleach.	Launder or dry clean according to instructions. Chlorine bleach may be used. Tumble or drip dry as desired. Safe ironing temperature, 320°F.

Federal Trade Commission's Generic Names	Trademark Names	Some Principal Uses in Home Furnishings	Characteristics	General Care Instructions
ACETATE (First produced in the USA in 1924)	Acele Ariloft Avicolor Aviso Celacloud Celacrimp Celafil Celaloft Celanese Celaperm Celarandom Celatow Celatress Celaweb Chromspun Estron Estron SLR Loftura Loftura Type F Type K	Draperies Lining fabrics Satin fabrics Faille fabrics Crepe fabrics Upholstery Taffeta fabrics Brocade fabrics Filling in comforters and pillows Lace Tricot fabrics	Has a luxurious hand. Drapes well. Economical. Able to be made in various lusters. Can take a wide range of colors. Shrink resistant. Poor abrasion resistance. Usually used where appearance is more important than durability.	Dry clean. Hand wash when indicated in lukewarm water. Press while damp on the wrong side at lowest setting. If finishing is required on the right side, use a press cloth. Acetate is adversely affected by certain solvents contained in such products as nail polish remover and perfumes.
TRIACETATE (First produced in the USA in 1954)	Arnel	Used where pleat or shape retention is important Textured knits Used in sharkskin, flannel, taffeta, jersey, and other popular fabric constructions	Shrink and wrinkle resistant. Resists fading. Easily washed. Abrasion resistance poor. Fabrics made from triacetate fibers can be softened by heat, and then shaped or pleated. After they are cooled, the shape or pleats are permanently set in.	May be laundered as directed. If ironing is desired, a high temperature setting may be used. Because triacetate fibers can stand such high temperatures, articles made from them require very little special care.
ACRYLIC (First produced in the USA in 1950)	A-Acrilan Acrilan Acrilan-Spectran Anywear Bi-Loft Chemstrand Colacril Creslan Orlon SEF Spectran Zefkrome Zefran II	Carpeting Blankets Draperies Fleece fabrics Pile fabrics Upholstery	Warm and lightweight with the feel of wool. Able to take bright colors. Keeps its shape. Resilient. Quick drying. Resists sunlight, weather, oil and chemicals. Good stability to repeated launderings. Rubbing causes tiny hairs on the fibers to bunch together into little balls or pills. Many fabrics made from acrylic fibers are soft, light, and fluffy.	For items that can be hand or machine washed, use warm water for both washing and rinsing. Add a fabric softener in the final rinse. Machine dry at a low temperature setting. Remove garments as soon as tumbling has stopped. If ironing is required use a moderately warm (never a hot) iron.

Federal Trade Commission's Generic Names	Trademark Names	Some Principal Uses in Home Furnishings	Characteristics	General Care Instructions
OLEFIN POLYPROPYLENE (Olefin first produced in the USA in 1949, Polypropylene introduced in 1961)	Herculon Marvess	Carpeting (largest single application) Nonwoven felts Carpet backing Indoor-outdoor carpeting Slipcovers Pile fabrics Upholstery	Very light in weight (Olefin fibers have the lowest specific gravity of all fibers). Able to give good bulk and cover. Abrasion resistant. Quick drying (fibers do not absorb moisture). Highly stain resistant. Resistant to deterioration from chemicals, mildew, rot, and perspiration. Strong. Very sensitive to heat. Weather resistant.	Stains on carpets containing Olefin fibers will usually blot away with an absorbent tissue. Machine wash in lukewarm water with a fabric softener added to the last rinse cycle. Machine dry at low setting only. Remove after tumbling has stopped. Do not use gas-fired dryers of the commercial or coin-operated type. If touch-up ironing is needed for articles containing a blend of fibers including Olefin, use the lowest possible temperature setting. Do not iron articles containing 100 per cent Olefin fibers.
POLYESTER (First produced in the USA in 1953)	Anavor Avlin Bi-Loft Blue "C" C Chemstrand Dacron Encron Esterweld Fiber 200 Fortrel Fortrel 7 Kodel Puff Stuff Quintess Spectran Super Stuff Tough Stuff Trevira Vycron	Permanent press merchandise Curtains Draperies Thread Carpeting Polyester fiberfill (a springy, lightweight nonallergenic, and nonmatting filling used in pillows, comforters, furniture, mattresses) Textured polyester fibers are used in woven and knit fabrics	Strong. Resistant to stretching and shrinking. Easy to dye. Resistant to most chemicals. Quick drying. Crisp and resilient when wet or dry. Wrinkle resistant— springs back into shape when crushed or twisted. Abrasion resistant. Able to retain heat-set pleats and creases. Easily washed.	Most items made from polyester can be machine washed in warm water. Add a fabric softener in the final rinse cycle. Machine dry at a low temperature setting, and remove articles from dryer when tumbling stops. For ironing, use a moderately warm (never a hot) iron.
SPANDEX (First produced in the USA in 1959)	Lycra	Upholstery and other articles where stretch is desired	Light in weight. Soft and smooth. Resistant to body oils. Stronger, more durable, and more powerful than rubber.	Care of upholstery products made with Spandex fibers depends on the blend. Follow instructions on label.

Federal Trade Commission's Generic Names	Trademark Names	Some Principal Uses in Home Furnishings	Characteristics	General Care Instructions
SPANDEX (*continued*)			Able to be stretched repeatedly and still recover to original length. Able to be stretched over 500 per cent without breaking. Abrasion resistant. Supple. Spandex does not suffer deterioration from perspiration, lotions, or detergents.	
GLASS (First produced in the USA in 1936)	Beta Fiberglas PPGC	Draperies	Not affected by moisture, sun, and most chemicals. Resists stretching. Dries quickly. Resists soil well. Excellent strength. Abrasion resistance poor. Nonflammable.	Hand or machine wash as directed. No ironing required.
NYLON (First produced in the USA in 1939)	Actionwear Anso Antron Astroturf Ayrlyn Bi-Loft Blue "C" Bodyfree C Cadon Cantrece Caprolan Captiva Cedilla Celanese Chemfit Chemline Chemlux Chemstrand Cordura Courtaulds Nylon Crepeset Crepeset Plus Cumuloft Enkaloft Enkalure Enkalure II Enkasheer Enkasheer Plus	Carpeting Upholstery Bedspreads Draperies Thread Curtains Stretch fabrics	Exceptionally strong. Elastic Abrasion resistant. Lustrous. Easy to wash. Resistant to damage from oil and many chemicals. Able to be dyed in a wide range of colors. Smooth. Resilient. Low in moisture absorbency. Filament yarns provide smooth, soft, long-lasting fabrics. Spun yarns lend fabrics lightweight warmth. Combines with many fibers to improve durability.	Most items made from nylon can be machine washed in warm water. A fabric softener should be added to last rinse cycle. Machine dry at a low temperature. Remove from dryer when tumbling stops. If ironing is required, use a moderately warm (never a hot) iron.

Federal Trade Commission's Generic Names	Trademark Names	Some Principal Uses in Home Furnishings	Characteristics	General Care Instructions
NYLON (*continued*)	Formelle Nomex Philips 66 Nylon Qiana Qulon Recall Shareen Speckelon Spectrodye II Stryton Twisloc Ultron Variline Vivana X-Static			
MODACRYLIC (First produced in the USA in 1949)	Acrilan Elura SEF Verel	Simulated fur Fleece fabrics Industrial fabrics Nonwoven fabrics Flame-resistant draperies and curtains Scatter rugs Carpets Institutional awnings and decorations	Wool-like hand. Resilient. Easy to dye. Abrasion resistant. Will not support combustion. Quick drying. Resistant to acids and alkalis. Shape retentive. Resists fading. Colorfast. Can be ironed at 150°F.	Deep pile articles should be dry cleaned or receive a fur cleaning process. Machine washable items should be washed in warm water, and a fabric softener should be added in the final rinse cycle. If machine dried, use a low setting and remove the articles as soon as tumbling stops. If ironing is required, always use a low setting.
METALLIC (First produced in the USA in 1946)	Lurex	Draperies Table linens Ribbons and braids Bedspreads Pillows Upholstery	Naturally stiff. Weak. Easily stretched. Won't tarnish. If suitably treated, not affected by climatic conditions.	150°F is safe ironing temperature.
SARAN (First produced in the USA in 1941)	Rovanna	Upholstery in public conveyances Deck chairs Garden furniture	Wears well. Resists common chemicals, sunlight, fading, staining, mildew, and the weather. Stiff and heavy. Nonflammable. Strength poor.	Can be ironed at 150°F.

For Your Bookshelf

The Reader's Digest Complete Do-It-Yourself Manual
The Reader's Digest Association (New York: 1973) The Reader's Digest Association Ltd. (London: 1969)

How to Do Almost Everything
by Bert Bacharach, Simon and Schuster (New York: 1970)

Painting, Plastering, Papering
Dell Publishing Co., Inc. (New York: 1967)

E-Z Decorating Tips
Banner Press, Inc. (New York: 1973)

Good Housekeeping Complete Book of Decorating
by Mary Kraft, Good Housekeeping Books (New York: 1971) Ebury Press (London: 1973)

The Money-Saver's Guide to Decorating
by Ellen Liman, Collier Books (New York: 1971) Collier-Macmillan Ltd. (London: 1971)

Buy It Right
by Jan Brown, Career Institute, Inc. (Mundelein, Illinois: 1973)

Picture Credits